MW01227607

Opera Omina

Vol. I

Amaarah Gray

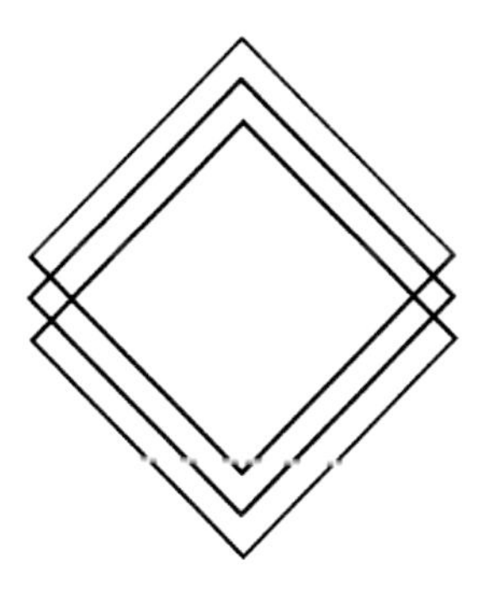

AMAARAH GRAY
PUBLISHING

For more information, address:
Amaarah Gray Publications,
P.O. Box 107,
Pacolet Mills, South Carolina 29373.

For my eggs.
May you never remain scrambled.

xXo

Antes

The mind is the most powerful, wonderful, horrible, dirty, pure system we maintain as a human being. The energy we exude. The silent moments that plague our thoughts in search of deeper meaning, praying we stumble onto life's purpose as if those pearls were even casted before swine to begin with. We are all here for the human experience. Souls existing in vessels living a human experience in order to learn, change, grow, and evolve into who we truly are meant to become.

In that order.

We rule our lives for the thrill, moving to feel something. In many instances, it's more like bobbing and weaving as we fight for our small moments in the sun, yet we are missing the memo.

We are here. The presence of our souls demand our epic best. It's the days that we fall short of that standard that can cause deep reflection as to where exactly we got our collective head so far up the fourth point of entry. Some get there quick. They stumble onto that small piece of pecking corn that gives them life's popcorn in abundance.

Others never get the illuminated lessons through the darkness. They remain blinded.

Those quiet moments are what teaches life's lessons as they hit you smack dab in the forehead. Before long, your spirit will question the cognitive thought swimming in your mental as you argue over useless, outdated facts.

What part do you play in other's consciousness?

Have you ever considered raising the rent on the space the ghosts from your past haunt, destined to keep you toxic, stuck, and unevolving?

As you try to rise and remain a sparkly example of a

triumphant human spirit earning the lessons via experience, you will start to realize that you are the problem.

Yes, *dear.*

You. Are. The. *Problem.*

While you contemplate the truth steaks of "why others simply won't allow you to be great", the glittery lightbulb moment shows up to render your Stevie Nicks dancing spirit useless as your mind goes on vacation for the foreseeable dimmed future.

Like a bar epic neon glowing sign, you see the four words looming toward you like a welcomed apocalypse rapture reckoning:

You are the solution.

Instead of grasping toward the truth, you scratch your head, doing Chinese arithmetic to make the chaos make sense.

The truth will indeed set you free, ruin your best lashes, make you sweat and smell like the outside; but first, it is gonna royally piss you off.

Nothing is worse than the second your cognitive thinking side kicks you in your perfectly contoured chin.

Toxicity is a learned behavior.

It's traditional, cultural, raw, gangster and pure belladonna wrapped up in the most delicious cinnamon sugar covered churro you've been served for decades. There's a reason that addiction to toxicity exists within your revolving Volvo hatchback. You've gotten used to existing in the pure poisoned powder.

In some cases, you've charmed, wined, and dined those toxic ways as you remain comforted in the thick of it all.

It's taught.

Pay close attention and reflect within.

Don't you dare reveal these moments that give you cause for pause. The backlash will greet you like an escaped convict. They will snitch, shank, and roll over on you.

Believe it and grab your razor.

Sometimes the toxicity has been introduced not your Howard the Duck lovin' innocence from a young age, unconsciously as those who inject your DNA with large quantities of grape peppered cyanide. They don't even realize that they, too, are card carrying residents of Toxicity.

These are folks who know no better.

Many things could be the culprit. Limited mindsets. Restricted, negative thinking. Mental abuse. Psychological problems. Shielded beliefs based on what others before them believed, experienced, considered, acted out, or thought as they led by example.

It's all there, fam.

The proof remains sauntering in the toxic, poisoned licorice pudding.

Whether or not you swallow what they spoon feed you daily, eventually that wild churro within you will question you during paused reflections based on your own human experience.

God bless those who remain unyoked and unwoke.

Their world remains unchanged, unwavering, stagnant, and closed to new movement.

It's the folks who are woke enough to know, confirm, and realize their toxicity, sneaky ambitions and regurgitations of traditional toxic traits, actions, beliefs, words, and poisoned close-minded, outdated perceptions that consciously continue the cycle of toxic within the confines of generational curses.

These individuals remain stuck, stagnant, unevolving while rejecting growth in every form as they constantly project and manipulate their toxic energy onto an innocent soul, who is willing to learn.

If it is you who allows what happens, you give them your power willingly.

That's why when you rise and make conscious efforts to regain your strength back, you must first take accountability as you claim back the power you allowed them to take from you. Through forgiveness, you call back all your pieces. You put yourself back together.

Not them.

They will reap what they sow.

Check.

There's absolute power in a name.

It's defining. Permanent. Overwhelming, at times. Controversial, depending on what you do with the name.

It's important.

Imperative.

Claiming.

Dominating.

It is deep and meaningful with ominous traditions seeped into every inch of your moniker. Identifying and solidified in documents that come with you home from the hospital.

Sometimes we love our given name.

Sometimes we loathe it, cowering at the mention of every syllable. What most miss is that it is you, the being, that gives your name power. Not others' perceptions of who they allow you to be.

Your name gives you meaning from the moment you take ownership of the name. It singles you out from the masses of souls who survive daily in the madness of this place. It is a name you build your whole life on. The words that make the love of your life's heart skip a beat at the mere whisper of it, inspiring lovesick emotion, and elation.

It can be generational. Sentimental as it can inspire reasons within another person to surface the minute your name lingers on their lips like a slow burning addiction or a poisonous infection, depending on their experience with you.

It is legendary as it is how you will pass on your legacy to your descendants.

Most importantly, your name is how your soul remains accountable for your sins when you leave this life for a more eternal existence, and you find yourself having to answer for all that was done as you lived this life as this person with that name.

For that reason, I am denying you my true name. I am every Hispanic woman who has dealt with the same measures in a roundabout way, in some texture, shape or form as explained in this Opera Omina.

While my name is wrapped in self-love at the moment, I, too, am numbered along the many of "mamas, mijas, baby, darling, sweetheart, kid, child and you's" that have been called every endearing moniker over a lifetime.

Over the span of my years, I was often identified as

"Muneca", which means "doll" in Spanish. Every instance in this Opera Omina has transpired. These are the lessons that followed.

If you find yourselves in these pages, don't trip. Take the lesson as they are laid out, learn, adapt, and grow. Take accountability and remember why your name was in the dish in the first place.

The ownership in your actions lies within the mention of your name.

When the chickens have begun clucking and finally remembered the way home to roost, you begin to wonder if their toxic chicken fight of a chess game was worth sacrificing their queen to gain notoriety for a series of complex disasters and a poisonous legacy that will follow their name for lifetimes.

When they come crowing, serve them as they've prepared their table before you.

Checkmate.

CHECKMATE

Chapter 1

In these streets.

There's hate in every family.

It's there. Secreted. Dressed up.

Often disguised as wisdom. It's traditional. Generational with an unfortunate repetitive circle. Like the graduation of outdated outlooks and poisonous perceptions of a generation who maintained different struggles we will never be able to stomach, let alone understand, experience, or survive.

It's biased, brazened, and unforgiving. It's a useful tactic of toxic, useless, yet acceptable excuses to allow their guilty views to infect the new crops of pure generational inspiration. No rest for wicked views, just as there is no justice for the pure thoughts in times of indifference.

No one speaks up about it.

No one questions why it is okay to replicate the hate or challenges the initial proprietor of loathing actions about their sickened views of the world. There are no inquiries into who positioned the disdain-filled etchings on the execrating glasses that shield their tired, uninspired, unambitious eyes from truly seeing the world as it is.

They've settled, surrendering the fight for righteousness in a sea of "I guess". Their boats of "good enough" has long overtaken their abilities for cosmic change and divine interjection.

It's all learned.

The behaviors we pass without consideration.

In These Streets

There's no mindful thought of trait placement once we start the process of procreation. We all wish we were that smooth.

We simply are not that skilled at over thinking, and not as control freaked as we'd claim to be. We probably should consider what legacy we are leaving behind right as the cycle starts, but that's not what happens. It would be nice to think someone thought enough of the world to begin with.

Maybe then the world we exist in wouldn't be in the state it is in.

The failures of learned behavior.

Young eyes witnessing toxic behavior. Examples. Demonstrations. Precedence. Pattern. Blueprint. Traditions.

That's how the world learns.

It's how babies learn everything. Everyone is taught how to do everything in life, except breathing, blinking, and swallowing. If those are the truest statements in this point of existence, why would anyone question how people become toxic?

The better question posed is, "how does someone know something is toxic?"

The answer . . . ***people point out the obvious.***

I found that answer out the day I stood at the edge of my egg donor donor's sidewalk with a gun pointed at my head at 7-years-old.

"Go ahead and try to leave. She won't live to see the next ten seconds," my egg donor donor's husky, cigarette dusted voice screamed toward my egg donors' egg donor.

Learned behavior strikes again.

He beat her for years. He stopped her from leaving that day. She suffered until the one day she threw a 50-inch television on top of him as he raised his hand to hit her.

She left the house and never looked back.

Thinking back on it now, I don't remember my grandmother smiling too much throughout life. She was always serious in expression. Exceedingly loving and kind to me, but never someone who appeared to have experienced joy in her life.

She was a strange character. A proud hen, if I ever saw one.

That much I knew from a very young age. She wasn't like everyone else. It didn't matter what it was, she always had to make sure I knew certain things that was expected of me.

"Always make your bed. If you make your bed, nice and neat, you won't want to go back to bed and you'll have to find more things to fill out your day, mama," she'd whisper out of her hushed breath as she smoothed out the knitted duvet that covered the bed we slept in.

"Okay, Eggy," I'd nod, watching every detail as she showed me her understanding of the world.

Totally not her name, but we will adapt to it as a shortened love moniker for egg donors' egg donor in this instance. Of course.

When you are small and things happen, you don't realize what kind of impact certain instances have in shaping your life. You don't realize how bad something is until the moment you see your Eggy cry.

You experience life as it comes to you with no

worries at that age.

Seven. The year sin starts counting-*allegedly*.

I never realized she wasn't happy.

Day in and day out, the woman I learned how to love from operated in routine. Waking up, she removed the rollers from her hair and made her rooster breakfast at 5 am. She'd do the dishes and call me to breakfast. We'd sit and I'd eat while she slowly sipped her coffee with a reflecting expression draped across her face.

If you were to read her non-verbal body language, her body would tell you the tension she housed was built up from years of being beaten badly, misused, and mistaken for a small glimpse of loving touches. The second her rooster would leave to work, her body would release, and she'd look over at me as if her expression said, "at last, we are free."

We would continue our day with Eggy changing into her chosen house dress, combing through the pin curls she styled her hair in. She'd effortlessly paint her lips with Avon's best reddest rouge, popping her lips as she patted them together.

Spraying her signature scent from a burgundy bottle with gilded letters spelling "Imari" written on the front, she'd breathe in and stare at herself in the mirror a moment as if she were confronting her inner demons.

Shrugging, she'd turn to leave in favor of hanging sheets to dry on the clothesline in the backyard.

"I don't care what you do in life. Whatever you do, do it with pride. Not just for you, but for your babies," she'd say, smoothing out the freshly washed sheets with her hands.

"I don't have babies, Eggy," I'd giggle, shaking my head as I handed her a clothespin from my pocket.

"You will one day, and let me tell you something else," she growled, grabbing my chin forcefully.

My alarmed eyes stared back up at her as my head tilted curiously.

"Never muddy your blood. I won't allow it and you will not like babies with hair like that," she exclaimed, grabbing her basket as she stormed inside the house.

At the time, I had no idea what she was talking about.

The first time she mentioned this, I was a Punky Bruster watching 7-year-old who thought boys were defective, demented, and mean. I was busy trying to eat my gummy bears and watch Alf. I had bigger things to worry about other than babies. I barely liked my baby doll. I would forget to feed her and often leave her in places like the bathroom shelf.

I was not in a mindset to consider what would happen if I actually had to be responsible for myself, let alone thinking of the state of future babies and the hair they may have.

Running my hands up and down the wet sheets as I ran back and forth between the lines of hung sheets, I wondered what happened to her to make her think such a thing.

"Why would I not want my babies having hair *"like that"*?" I'd whisper to myself, wondering if there was something she knew but chose not to share. "*Wait-* hair like *what*?"

Eggy and I had no secrets.

She told me all sorts of things. As far as I knew, she

was the wisest person I knew up to that point. In my eyes, Eggy was a superhero that was right up there with Jem and Shera. She was the best tortilla making Thundercat I ever knew.

We were tight. She would never withhold anything from me.

I shared all my favored snacks with her.

Walking back toward the house, I picked up a broken twig of a branch, flicking it side to side across my legs until I got closer to the house. Flicking it one last time, I threw the branch aside as I walked in through the back door. Glancing around the kitchen, I breathed in deeply as the aroma of garlic flavored butter beans wafted through the air.

No one cooks as good as Eggy.

One thing you can always be sure of was that when you stayed at Eggy's house, you were going to be eating good. That particular day, we were going to be eating carne guisada, beans, rice with homemade tortillas, served with an iced cup of sweet tea.

God, how I miss those days.

She had this way of making her tortillas. They were the best I've ever eaten. She'd often have to make dozens because there was a point in the night before dinner that she'd never be able to get one tortilla in the warming dish towel she'd set up to keep her freshly made tortillas warm. As soon as that tortilla was taken off the fire, I'd be standing front and center with a spoonful of butter at the ready.

Those truly were the best days of my life.

Right off the kitchen, there is this stone wall that

had a loose stone within the wall. It was my hiding place for items like quarter sticky putty, my favorite Barbie shoes or even candy I wanted to save and secret away from my evil little half-chick.

From the day she was born, I knew she was a poisoned egg.

Rotten from inside the uneven yoke out.

I said what I said. Argue with your egg donor.

It's the truth.

Grabbing my sticky silly putty from my secret hiding place, I smacked my fingers back and forth on the sticky, gelatin feeling surface as I skipped the short distance from the kitchen through the hallway to her original bedroom. As I walked into her room, I found her sitting down on her bed, staring out of the window as if she were lost in thought.

"Eggy?" I called, gently knocking on the open door.

I didn't dare ask what she was thinking about. It wasn't my 7-year-old business. What I was more plagued with was why my babies couldn't have "hair like that".

When I finally called her attention back from wherever her mind drifted to, she released a small, yet kind wry smile in my direction, raising her hand out.

Grabbing her hand, I climbed up on the bed to sit down next to her with my pigtails smacking my face.

Sitting quietly a moment, I bounced my feet off the edge of the bed.

"Get me something from the closet, will you?" she asks, pointing to her closet. "It's down there on the right side. Be careful. It's heavy."

Shaking my head yes, I jumped off the bed. I didn't

know what she was asking for. All I knew is that she asked me to do something. Not wanting to make her upset, I was going to do whatever she asked.

I probably would have robbed a bank for her had she asked.

Eggy was ride or die.

One crazy thing about my Eggy's closet, it had a bazillion items within the small confines of the 11 x 11 space. The woman had clothes for years, yet she'd still only wear the same old raggedy house dresses. Don't get me wrong. Her house dresses weren't discolored, nor did they have any holes in them.

If they did, she'd whip out her smallish sewing kit from the old cookie tin she kept and close said hole immediately. She had fancy dresses a typical Hispanic Eggy would have.

Church dresses. Slacks that paired well with decorative, seasonal sweaters that often featured a broach of some sort.

All items wrapped in dry cleaning plastic.

Her side was on the right. His was on the left.

Her shoes were something else.

She had pairs of the same design in shoes. Low wedged heels that went with every item in her wardrobe. Egg Donor sandals sold by Payless Shoes. She had her chosen color of black in matte finishes and every so often, there would be a patent leather shiny pair that noted the importance of Christmas or some cousin's wedding as that was the only time she'd ever bust out the church wear.

Cruising to the right pocket of her closet beyond the miles of the same design of pocketbooks or "bolsa" as she would often call them. They were old and often worn out, but the woman would just refuse to throw them out. Deep down she knew she would never use them again, but she had an issue with throwing out perfectly good bolsas.

How dare we'd even think such a thing?

The audacity.

The nerve.

I wasn't sure if she was under the impression that I had mind reading power techniques at 7-years-old, but every single time she asked me to get anything out of that closet, it was always the same sort of wishful introduction.

"Get me something from the closet, will you?"

Famous last words.

"Eggy, what am I even searching for?" I'd holler.

"You'll know when you see it," she'd giggle back.

"I'll know when I . . . oh?" I breathe, exhaling when I laid eyes on the thing her soul was calling for.

There beyond her secreted boxes of saltines, cracker jacks and gram crackers that she kept hidden in her closet was the oldest glass piggie banks that stem from somewhere back in the 1930s. They were the most beautiful, blackened grayish hammered glass banks that were filled to the brim with quarters, dimes, nickels, and pennies.

Not mixed in disarray.

Each bank had its own organized coin. Eggy had this thing about mixing the coins. I just could not wrap my mind around it all.

The way I saw it, those were coins that could be spent on candy. My eyes swirled with opportunity as I pictured what kind of small fortune I had in front of me, which could, *of course*, afford all the Super Bubble my sweetened heart could want.

We were RICH!

At least, I thought so.

"No, we are not *rich*. You don't spend these coins," she'd scoff, removing a bobby pin from her hair.

Placing the bobby pin into the narrow slot of the bank, grandma attempted to remove a few coins from the safe harbor in the sea of coins. Everything inside my tiny frame wanted to bash the old bank to the floor, grab the coins into my hands like a maniacal pigtailed gum baron and run for the nearest Circle K to make all my 7-year-old Violet Beauregard dreams come true.

The sweetness of that gum.

I swear its kid crack, created to overtake the minds of the richest coin bubble gun goblins this side of Texas. The best flavor of Super Bubble, at the time, was the green. A close second in my opinion was the grape but pink Super Bubble has a piece of my soul.

Either way, argue with your egg donor.

I know my worth in Super Bubble weight.

No mistakes were made.

Moving on.

I think she could tell I wanted to smash her banks. Her mischievous smirk told me she knew exactly what color my soul was painted in.

"Never smash these banks," she reasoned, removing one coin after another with each swipe of the bobby pin.

"Whaa- *me?* Why would I do such a thing, Eggy?" I

ask, clutching my sticky silly putty as if she wounded me with her violating assumption.

"*Mmhmm.* These are incredibly old. My mama gave them to me when I was little. She taught me to save my money, just like I am teaching you," she exhaled, running her hand over the small coin fortune that now dotted her bed in shimmery perfection.

Laying my head on the edge of the bed as I kneeled watching her roll up the coins into penny rolls the bank gave her, I ran my small index finger over the surface of her spilt quarters.

"Eggy, you said they are old. What's Jesus like?" I ask, poking fun at her age. "Does he like gummy bears?"

"He's nice. You'd like him," she'd snap back, snickering as she slammed the end of her rolled coins on the nightstand located beside her bed. "He steals your gummies when you sleep."

Giggling, I'd pull more coins to me.

After several trips back to her hidden trove she called her closet for more penny rolls, I worked up enough nerve to ask her what she meant about my hair.

My hair, for the record, is fabulously kinky, thick, and extremely curly. It has been glamored by the sun and depending on what the humidity is like in Texas, I might just appear like I've been electrocuted by the sun's rays with no moisture to be left within these curls.

I can make my hair afro with the best of 'em. Beautifully round and bountiful. I love my hair. It takes an extreme amount of product, conditioner and praying to get this curly realness tamed to resemble a person under this sea of curly thickness.

In These Streets

The Indian in my blood is prime and present within the ancestral appearance of my hair.

If I ever allow it to grow long enough, I'd be straight up painting with all 1200 colors of the doggone wind.

If it truly were higher the hair, closer to God up in here, I'd be right up there with Jesus himself. Still ain't sharing my gummy bears. Not for all the Super Bubble in Texas. No mistakes would be made.

I am as God made me.

Thinking over her words, I just could not shake her statement. I'm sure she had to have said it at some other point, but this particular day, I must've been paying close attention as that is the day I identify with the beginning of her toxic programming.

The way my mind saw it, when the bible described Jesus, it said he had hair with a texture like wool. If my guy had that kind of hair texture, I was in good company as far as my 7-year-old self was concerned. Gummies be damned.

Jesus' hair rocks.

Mine must be in good favor.

I didn't think there was anything wrong with my hair, other than when my egg donor would comb through it and pull it. Turns out, she pulled it while combing it because she was a whole evil, toxic, horrid bitch of a hen, not because of the texture.

Believe me, she has earned that title.

The more you know.

Something in my soul was stirring because her statement had me thinking she knew I was out back making mud pies in my dress, which is a definite no-no for a lady.

Moving my hair out of my face, I looked up at her and gathered every ounce of courage I had available.

"Eggy, earlier when you said not to muddy my blood, what did you mean?" I questioned, bracing myself for impact.

Eggy never got mad at me. Never raised her voice. She was exceedingly kind and the total opposite of my egg donor, which is a whole different story, made for another book once I've had enough tequila to drown the wounds that evil travesty put in place.

Born in 1932, Eggy came from a different time.

She was a woman who didn't have much education as she left home early after she jumped into her rooster's car after a sock hop and refused to leave. I'm pretty sure there is more to the story they gave me, but from what I was told, her rooster met her at the sock hop, danced with her for two dances and was ready to leave. As he was leaving, she jumped into his car, so he agreed to drive her home.

When he pulled up to the house, her egg donor said they had to marry because he brought her home.

They didn't know each other whatsoever.

Eggy was a whole savage firecracker.

If only she knew then what she was getting herself into.

"What do you mean?" she answered, placing her banks back into her treasure trove of a closet.

"I mean what I said. You told me not to muddy my blood. I don't know what that means, Eggy," I countered, holding court.

Sitting down on her bed, she exhaled as she prepared her thoughts. It occurred to me at this point that she wasn't sure I was hearing what she said. Strange as it sounds, I idolized the woman.

I would do whatever she said because she said it.

Eggy's word was bond.

"It means you are not to bring home anyone who has skin darker than yours," she advised, serious in tone. "If you did, we'd hang you from your toes on that tree out there."

Confused, I looked at her trying to figure out where she was going with this.

For as long as I have been alive at this point, the point to never bring anyone home with me hand been drilled into my head as if they would ever let me out of their sight.

I was seven.

The only thing I was bringing home with me was Super Bubble and a swift confession after I rob my grandmother of her small coin oil fortune hiding in her closet.

"Why would I bring them home? Where would they sleep?" I added, elated that she didn't realize I would get my tail tied in a knot if anyone stayed over without asking first.

It's like she went to sleep and forgot what a terrible person her egg, my egg donor, grew into being. She knew what she raised. There was no misconception in the travelers allowed in our joint.

It stemmed from a world of mommy dearest filled "not gonna happen".

"That's not what I mean. You'll understand when you are older," she exhaled, sounding more exhausted with the release of every breath.

Truth be told, her rooster was so dark, the only way you could find him in the dark was by the gleam of the gold tooth with a diamond in his dentures. Of all the shelled turtle calling the armadillo shelled nonsensical things, it seems she was not the authority on pigmented skin.

For the record, I still don't understand, and I am 40.

That's how racism starts- *in my opinion.*

At 7-years-old, I wasn't thinking about "muddying my blood". I wasn't considering who I was bringing home for whatever reason. I wasn't thinking about including anyone in my Super Bubble fortune.

Not allowing a small glimpse of a future-filled vision into anyone having a lifetime pass into my pillow fort.

My 7-year-old mind had bigger fish to fry with those tortillas slathered in butter that awaited me in a few hours. I had zero thoughts involving the muddying f any life substance. I'd like to be able to say that I would never hear those harmful, directive words strung together to program my young subconscious again after this first instance, but if I did, I would be wrong.

Eggy had a way with her perception. Strong in her faith but loyal to her beliefs, she was going to ensure that I got the mothering she felt I lacked. She wanted for me to know how important it was that I was a girl.

While she loved her sons dearly, she wasn't so close with my egg donor. There are many numerous reasons to unpack as to why, but that is another series for another time. As a family friend would later tell me, I got the egg donor my always wanted, stationed within Eggy.

"Always paint your nails. A lady always has her nails painted to catch the eyes of others," she'd tell me as she sipped her coffee. "Never chew your nails. That's how you get sick."

Nodding, my eyes would inspect my nails to find there was not an ounce of color to be found. It's almost like she was always trying to confuse my tiny mind yet enlighten me to the ways of a woman.

I didn't find out there were different sorts of women until I went across the street to sit with the neighbor, Mrs. Z. At this time, I can't remember why I went over there. I am not sure if my grandma had an appointment or what the actual reason I was there in the first place.

Scandal would tell you in later years of a rumor that Eggy was having some affair with a plumber rooster, who found his way to tidy her pipes quite often.

I was told I met him a few times.

If I am being honest and of a pure heart, I don't remember any plumber dude named Joe. I remember meeting so many of her so-called friends. They'd come over and gossip as I stole pieces of sponge cake or donuts that Eggy would go pick up from Fiesta, the world's best bakery, to have with their gossip filled coffee hour.

It was the best.

Clucking hens.

I'd listen to their tornado-filled Texanized version of Spanish and broken English tell a slanted version of the truth about all sorts of people we knew and even a few we knew nothing of. As big as our city was, it was small considering the people we all knew. Everyone knew everyone because everyone and their mothers went to the same high school.

There were only three main schools that rivaled each other that people went to.

In one way or another, everyone eventually crossed everyone's path.

If they didn't, you might have met these hollering, clucking hens at church, a church function, fiesta, a barbeque, a baby shower, or someone's debut otherwise known as a "quinceanera".

In most ways, if you were someone like me, you met these other folks by going with your egg donor's egg donor to visit friends, cousins, sisters, or past neighbors they stayed in touch with.

Best believe all your business was on front street with old coconut wireless over there amidst the hen squakwing.

I sat quietly, eating my sugar cookies as I listened to why my grandma couldn't stand someone because of how they made and ate their potato salad, which turned out to have a totally different meaning entirely.

Leave it to Eggy and her clucking friend to talk in code. I always did know exactly what they were saying. I was a puzzle wizard, especially if idle gossip was to be had.

Back at Mrs. Z's house, there was never any telling what might await you. She was fun and scary at the same time. She had the appearance of an exceedingly aged Rizzo mixed in with Spanish textures of Charro. Her rooster loves her more than life itself.

Thinking of them now, I could swear up and down those two were Greek with the way they got on, but as it turns out, they stem from Monterrey, Mexico; or something like that.

Rooster fighting chickens with sharp talons.

Mrs. Z's front yard looks like a home that started out in Farmville before the owner started to learn how to play. It's a colorful, prize-positioned forest that has big dream ambitions to grow into a mock garden of Eden.

Anything to get the notoriety of the cluckity-cluck-cluck.

It's the kind of yard you'd rush tc the door, knocking while praying that a snake didn't up and snap at you as you tried to gain entrance.

This woman was always so nice to me. She talked funny with the rhythm of her words. Super-fast, bunched but somehow she always explained herself well. She was aweinspiring. That's for sure.

Mrs. Z had a huge personality that could take over any area within a 20-mile radius. Her voice boomed and she had a remarkable, full-bodied laugh.

As amazing as that sounds, that's not what thrilled me about her. I want to say she had some sort of stammer, where her words turned into thoughts too quickly in her mind, tripping up her tongue at times when the excitement of her guided directives were about to dance out of her person. She was something epic.

Mrs. Z reminded me of an extreme Hispanic version of Eartha Kitt, the original cat woman.

If Eggy had a treasure trove of a closet, Mrs. Z had a room that looked like the inner workings of a dry cleaner's main floor. Ceiling to floor. Left to right. Top to bottom. Rows and rows of clothes that were hung on makeshift racks.

Truth be told and set us free, Mrs. Z had an organized hording issue.

Located in the center of the room was this old school circle mirrored vintage vanity. Every time I came over, Mrs. Z would sit me down next to her at her vanity as she lit her eyeliner on fire with an old rusted over metal flip lighter. Blowing the flame out, she'd make her plumped lips into an "o" shape, carefully placing what she considered a beauty mark of a Marilyn mole above her lip, two inches away from her nostril. Sometimes it was on the left.

Later in life, I discovered it depended on the mood she was in. If she were feeling saucy and entertaining, that Marilyn mark would be adorning the right side of her face.

I always wondered if she ever got nuts enough to place more than one Marilyn.

Everything she did was like watching an old telenovela, where the Ursula type of villain paint herself into a cascade of colors as she seduced herself through the reflection staring back at her. She was a trip.

"I paint myself for myself. Not for any man. You remember this. *Yes*?" her smokey voice would advise.

"Yes! Does your husband like the war paint?" I'd ask, giggling as she wiggled her eyebrows at herself.

Opening the Avon lipstick, a shade she no doubt ordered from Eggy, she rimmed her lips like she was painting the drapes that lined her soul. Mrs. Z. was serious about her war paint.

"Do you know why we call this war paint, muneca?" she'd ask, painting the room in powerful radiance.

"Because you paint your lips like you're painting a house?" I laughed, playing with one of twenty creepy dollies that she had draped in crochet realness. "I don't use that stuff."

"It's because we use, *this stuff*, to go to war with the men," she'd growl, forcibly closing the lid on her lipstick. "We hypnotize them, then hang them by the toes."

"O-*kay*, Mrs. Z. Can I have a grilled cheese?" I muster, placing the doll down back in its place.

I didn't need to know why we were all the sudden battling men. As far as I knew, Wonder Woman and the Amazonians had us covered. We didn't need to be painting our faces with battle paint as long as her lasso was still in play. I also couldn't help but wonder how long it would take their toes to separate from the rest of their body.

Mrs. Z knew more than she let on about said man war.

That much I knew.

Sitting in her kitchen, I looked around as I sat on an old stool stationed beside the stove. I am not certain if it was because her house was different from Eggy's, but everything inside Mrs. Z's home looked like it belonged in a museum.

The typical plastic covering the sofas in the sitting room that squeaked weird were glistening from the sunlight that secreted its way through the forest she called a front yard, catching my eye at just the right time. It was never awesome sitting on those couches.

Not only did you burn every inch of the back of

your legs as you sit down, but there is also never a way to ensure that you didn't sound like you released an epic fart, sitting on one of her couches.

It was horrible and awesome wrapped up in an amazingly human experience.

You have not lived until you've been embarrassed by the hot plastic sounding fart machine of a couch plastic Spanish folks have in their home.

"How many you want? One or two?" she'd push, grabbing my chin.

"Two," I answer, honking her nose.

"Coming up," she'd wink, turning to make my sandwich.

Turning up her favorite Tejano station, KEVA, Mrs. Z would hum along to the sounds as she cooked, rotating her gaze between my position and the sizzling wonderful she was cooking in the hot cast iron skillet.

Seizing the opportunity, I sought out an answer to the plaguing question in my mind.

"Mrs. Z . . .?" I began, clearing my throat as she led me over to the kitchen table.

"Yes?" she hummed, placing the plate down in front of me.

Turning her back toward me, she walked over to the fridge, grabbing a class cup stationed in the rack on the counter. Pouring some milk into the glass, Mrs. Z. kicked the fridge door closed with her foot as she walked back toward the table.

"What does muddying your blood mean?" I quizzed, taking a bite of my crispy grilled cheese sandwich.

I should've known with the way her mouth went agape that it wasn't exactly something that must be mentioned in polite grilled cheese conversation.

"*Er-* Who. Who told you this, muneca?" she countered, crossing her hands in front of her on the table.

"Eggy," I answer between bites. "She mentioned it when we were hanging the sheets."

Mrs. Z. raised her eyebrows like she was trying to get them to dance of her face. Clearing her throat, she got up from her seat to get herself a glass of water. Turning around to face me as she stood at the sink, she clinked her teeth before answering.

"Listen to me very closely, huh?" she exhales, putting her hand out.

I shook my eager head yes.

If there was truth to tell, Mrs. Z. was not going to let me down. She'd give it to me straight. She'd let me know what was up in the big, stinking mud comment.

"I don't-" she began, grabbing the bridge of her nose. "I am not . . . listen, don't date a Puerto Rican. Okay?"

Scrounging my nose, I unleashed an epic expression of concern in her direction.

"Do what?" I managed, more confused than when I started to ask.

"They are mean. They don't like candy and they smell like a distillery. Eat your food. It'll be time for dinner before you finish, ah?" she hissed, pushing my plate toward me.

Eating my crispy grilled cheese, my mind began to wonder what made these ladies have such an opinion. Thoughts swarmed around my head like I was struggling to find air-filled clarity dipped in truth for once. They eat all the candy. Could a person eat that much candy and live to tell the tale?

By the end of my grilled cheese, one thing was clear:

I will not be sharing any of my candy . . . with anyone.

Feeling more confused than when I began my righteous search for the meaning behind the statement, I wondered if I would ever marry anyone to begin with. So far, I witnessed the exchange between my own egg donor's donors, which were the basis of relationships this far.

Eggy woke up, painted her face, unwound her curlers into a curly crown of darkened pin curls before she began her day of cooking, cleaning and being what she believed to be the essence of a woman.
Sometimes she cried when she thought no one was the wiser, but my eyes saw the pain.

I personally never saw him hit her. I only saw the crying aftermath that was filled with overturned items and a spilled mess of limited, dying ambition.

Over the years, she would fill my mind with small bits of secreted knowledge.

I never did find out what muddying your blood meant until the age of 27.

After being hounded to find and research the bloodline, I was knee deep in old church registries with Eggy sitting across from me as life came back to gut check her into the travesty of a lifetime in her era.
The way she used that phrase, it came from her parents.

It was a learned perception that was drilled into her mind.

In These Streets

Being born in 1932, Eggy had a whole lot of outdated misconceptions that were instilled in who she was forced to be, not who she was meant to become. Back then, race was a huge issue, especially being that her father was of Spanish descent.

Spanish as in Spaniard.

It's not how it sounds. The man appeared Caucasian with the blues eyes anyone could see for miles. The darkness of your skin was a huge thing for him. I am not sure why. By the time I was old enough to understand him, he talked so soft and usually remained silent until he had something profound to say.

He, too, lived a life of scandal.

It is not my job to judge, I just find life dripping in irony as I am the one who is the recent recipient of his poisonous outlook via his egg.

I am profoundly happy to say those outlooks end with me.

I've always told my own children that they should be proud of who they are, who they love and where they come from as these things tend to make you who you are as a person, but they don't always contribute to who you have yet to become.

Circumstances change you.

Whether you like them or not.

Same can be said about enlightenment.

Once you gain knowledge on certain situations, you can't just go back to not being the wiser.

Knowledge changes perception, outlook, and feelings.

Just like it did the day I found the beginning of our

bloodline.

Flipping through the church records that started in 1532, I carefully ran my gloved fingers over the records that held many families that began through this church. Part of me was so excited to be starting history directly in the face as I searched for traces of the past. Times were different then.

People in the mission during this time in history were forced to marry, convert to Catholicism, and even forced to conceive by violent methods.

"Eggy, do you think they loved each other?" I asked, carefully flipping the page.

"What's love got to do with anything?" she countered, taking a deep breath.

Looking up at her from the huge registry I held, I could tell the bitterness was swirling to the surface.

"What do you mean?" I breathed, glancing toward a passerby.

"That's not how it was done in those days. It was a different time. People in the mission were told who they were to marry. Not everyone married for love you know," she explained, dropping her eyes.

Knowing Eggy's history, I knew it was best to tread lightly on this issue.

"Okay," I nodded, returning my attention back to the records.

It was clear that this whole situation was bothering her spirit as I could see her fidgeting her life away in my peripheral vision. Clearing my throat, I seized the opportunity for an answer to my life's burning question right as I landed on the church records that validated our bloodline.

"Eggy, why have you always told me not to muddy my blood?" I inquired, looking up while pressing my index finger to the entry so I didn't lose my place.

Eggy glanced around as if to see who heard my query, crossing her hands on the table. Moving her hand in a dusting motion, grandma ran her aged hand over the surface of the table like she was smoothing out not so proud wrinkles in time.

"Eggy?" I pushed.

Closing her eyes, she released an exhale that seemed like it stemmed from her soul.

"Come on, Eggy. I got to know. I have to know. What's up? Why did you say that? I've always wanted to know. I asked several people throughout my life and no one would friggen say a word other than what they prefer me not to date. No one ever said why. Be honest," I added, raising my brows.

"I told you that since you were little because I didn't want that for you," she answered, pulling her purse closer to her.

Eggy often pulled her purse closer to her when she was feeling triggered. Part of me didn't want her to feel personally attacked. The other, more demanding part of me wanted my answer.

It's not like I didn't know what her statement meant.

Muddying your blood means that you actively choose to date, marry, or breed with someone of African American or mixed blood descent.

It's hateful.

It's wrong in my opinion and this is the exact type

of thing that happens in Hispanic families.

I want to be clear- it may not happen in every, single family, but it is happening. People just refuse to confirm the truth.

It's odd.

They don't want to be seated with the reputation of the type of people who would say or hold their family to those standards, yet they don't do anything to change that aspect of expectation within themselves.

Racism is not acceptable in any form, by any individual.

Hate is taught by example. If you set that toxic behavior and drill it into a young person's mind like it is tradition, why would you expect for that person not to grow up teaching the same nasty expectations to their kin?

If we are a product of our raising, at what point does a person say, "enough is enough. It ends with me."

This was where I drew my line in the sand.

I didn't want to pass that same, vapid minded traditional expectations on to my kids. I want them to be free to love who they love with no limitations, expectations, restrictions, or conditions.

Add those things in- that's not love.

You love who you love.

Gay, straight, Bi, black, white, polka dotted people, if that suits your fancy.

After all I've lived through, I was sure about one thing in my life when it came to my kids. I was going to love them as they are, for whom they are as they choose to live. It's not my job to tell them who to love. It is my job to not just tell them how to love with an open heart, but to show them as I love them completely to the best of my ability and accept them as God sent them to me.

This way, they too, will pass down my tradition of newly established love to my descendants and so on.

I've always made it a point to be as open as I can with my children, giving them a truthful explanation, so that they are aware.

Even if they ask after my sins, I give them the truth to gain understanding while also providing what I learned from my perspective so they can make their own perspective and understanding something they have formed without preconceived bias involved.

I grew up different.

It wasn't from traditions that toxic city taught me. It was from the example they established, drilling it into my head in the form of pain.

At one point or another, you as a young Hispanic female will be told who you are expected to date, how you are expected to dress and conduct yourself- if your family is anything like mine.

"You didn't want what for me?" I pushed once more.

If she was finally talking and explaining everything, I wanted the answers I may never receive again.

"I don't want people looking at you . . . the way people look at people who muddy their blood. The way the hair comes out. The baby would have a hard life. People aren't nice," she said, explaining the best way she can.

Eggy wasn't exactly a wordsmith when it came to explaining her reasoning behind her feelings that are usually wrapped up in belief. The problem is those beliefs she clings to with her old, weathered yet experienced hands are formed with toxic views of a city that no longer exists.

It wasn't until that moment where my finger held my place on that family registry that history dealt Eggy a hard lesson.

I had never been so fulfilled in my whole life.

Coming from a family who often spoke behind closed doors in very colorful language when it came to folks different from our kin, I had never been so excited to unveil that piece of hidden history.

"What do you mean, "people aren't nice", Eggy? This is America. People are people," I exhaled, allowing my eyes to memorize my findings.

"Ay. You know what I mean," she hissed, holding tighter to her purse.

"Welp, I guess you best get used to it then, Eggy. We with our people now," I countered, placing the book in front of her.

Pointing to the entry dated circa 1532, I held my finger there for her to read. Adjusting her glasses, Eggy cleared her throat as her eyes widened when she read the enlightening line.

There comes a time in everyone's life that will teach you why it is imperative to never teach hateful things. Whether they choose to admit and accept what God teaches them along the way is up to that person. When the moment arises, we owe it to fate to accept, comprehend the lesson and adapt in gratitude.

Some take the lesson when it comes.

Others refuse and end up doomed to repeat it.

Taking a huge deep breath in, grandma opened her purse, pulling out a cherry lifesavers from her half-eaten pack. Only the Lord knows how long the pack had been in her purse. Like many of her generation, Eggy never wanted to throw anything away.

I cringed a tiny fraction, furrowing my eyebrows toward her as I wondered if that stale candy plastic taste was assaulting her taste buds as we sat there. Sad to report, I was not brave enough that day to taste what was left of that lifesaver rainbow.

She was just gonna have to endure that torture on its own.

I waited with eager anticipation for her reaction.

As selfish as it sounds, I wanted her response to be one of compassion and understanding. The "I told you so" part of my heritage wanted to point to the line and let out a victorious, villainous, exaggerated laugh as I jumped on the table in that library and hollering, "see what hate gets you?", but the more rational part of my heart that was in control knew she didn't understand.

Sometimes words fall on deaf ears no matter how you dress them up.

"What does that say?" she whispered, looking left and right before pointing to the book.

Shaking my head at her, I let out a small, disapproving sigh as I walked from my side of the table to hers.

"It says that our ancestor, which is listed right here in the registry of the church, is of mestiza blood. This is the church registry from 1532. That right there is the very beginning of our bloodline, grandma. It's where we started," I answer, waiting for my words to reach her.

"Mestiza?" she queried, running her fingers over the entry.

"Well, yeah," I nod. "Mestiza."

"Yes," she fumes, clearing her throat.

"Yessss," I reiterated, giving her a concerned glance in return.

She always disliked when we said "yeah".

She claimed it showed no home training.

"This is the start of our blood?" she polled, flipping the page.

"Well, what's recorded anyway. I'm sure there are other folks in the lineup somewhere. We aren't plants. We didn't just show up through osmosis, grandma," I smirked, cowering when she smacked my hand.

A small, secreted smile escaped her lips as she continued reading.

"More than likely, this is probably the branch that came over from the old country with the church. Could be that's why," I added, writing my discovery.

I proudly smiled, releasing a small laugh as I cleared up the stacked books.

"Why are you laughing?" Eggy asked, following me around the library.

Throwing my fist in the air, I closed my eyes, grabbing my chest proudly.

"I'm with my people now. I always knew we had mestiza blood. You can't tell me nothin', Eggy. My blood been muddy since 1500's. Seems to me your people had some explaining to do," I explained, doing a small victory dance.

Clutching her purse closer to her chest, Eggy looked around to see who was watching. She was always excessively big on what other people thought about our family. I didn't care as much.

I was more concerned with the notion that every single person in said bloodline held the same tired, outdated outlook as my library record hunting companion. The child inside trying to tread water in the sea of righteousness wanted to poke fun at the rest of the family for maintaining that same brand of dislike, but I kept my party inside.

God has a way of getting folks to be more accepting. I figure it's because you just can't saunter into Heaven being your hateful self.

There's no room for that sort of nonsense in there. You can't party with people you despise for something that is not in their control.

For someone who is raised to know that God is love and that is how you are to treat one another, she had a few of her facts assbackward.

That is why it is important to address whatever you're at odds with from the jump. Later you won't have so many things to atone for once your time comes.

After in-depth research for a genealogy project, I found out that many of the ancestors we stemmed from were raped by slaves that came over with the Spanish conquistadors.

Once the women were dealt with in that regard, they were often forced into marriages by the priests within the missions as if that were going to settle the score and vindicate their suffering.

I'm still a bit salty about it for my people, the brave ancestors who dared to survive such a time, but since when has history ever been kind to those who have suffered injustices at the hands of another.

Given the opportunity to live during a situation like that, I don't think I would have been able to thrive under such conditions myself.

The newfound information made that blood muddying situation rest in an instant. It didn't make it right, just as it didn't settle any wrongs. It clarified why that saying was introduced into the family to begin with.

The record we were reading was that of my Eggy's egg donors' egg donor. It wasn't so far removed from where we were as I was third generation. Her mother and father apparently introduced that toxic doctrine into her like it was the 11th commandment.

She, in-turn, continued the tradition to her own kids and because I was always with Eggy, she tried to poison the well with me by continuing the intellectual shade branding.

As I said before, I made it a point to ensure that this toxic trait ended with me. I didn't want to box my children in. I didn't want to continue the same toxic poisonous view that would hinder any aspect of their lives, especially when it comes to dictating who they love.

People love who they love.

Love is color blind.

It's genderless.

It's supposed to be unconditional.

It wasn't until many years later after many healing experiences that I am able to see where the hate stemmed from. I see how the outlook was created and after being enlightened I see the why in her perception.

If experience is what shapes us as human beings, then understanding the experiences is up to us in order to grow. I've tried to explain the same notions to my grandmother until I was blue in the face. Eventually, I had to surrender to indifference and let that war go.

It was not until I caught her trying to fill my children with some of her toxic knowledge that I realized her hate was a chosen outlook.

When I confronted her right then about her actions, trying to get her to be accountable for her own hateful outlook, all she replied with was, "I'm old. You can't be mad at me."

Her outlook is outdated and unacceptable. It's an outlook that spreads racism, hate and disloyal traits to new, young minds.

It's also one I was not willing to entertain by any means.

As old as she is now, she'd never be able to understand life as it adapts daily.

Her biggest gripe when I was coming up was the consistency of my hair and the thickness of my blood, so to speak. I wasn't surprised a bit when she considered my best friend at the time my girlfriend as in life partner, not childhood friend.

My friend, at the time, did not fit the usual female description her brain sustains. She had tattoos everywhere and an edge hairstyle that had one side shaved with the rest of her hair being fashioned into a man's type of short haircut.

It didn't matter to grandma that my so-called friend had just cut her hair that way after trying to prove a point to the guy who subsequently left her for his ex-girlfriend, a woman who was bisexual but appeared like a man with the same haircut.

After a meltdown, that friend claimed she could do the hairstyle better than anyone, so she cut her hair off in the same style.

That hair paired with the tattoos everywhere and a sheltered outlook meant that Eggy was once again holding on tight to those hateful beliefs.

To this day, she still believes that was my person.

I didn't have the heart to tell her the true reason that friend was there in the first place, but that is another story for another book.

The point of this experience in life is to be very careful of the outlook and perceptions you entertain. If you are afraid to adapt and accept change as it comes to your doorstep, you just might find yourself in a muddy blooded situation as you are forced to explain your hate to a new generation.

Hate takes many forms.

It's in tradition.

Often times, it's hidden within culture. Deeply seeded within people we'd trust our lives to. The changes this world desperately needs lies within the very capable minds of new generations.

There is no room in this world for outdated views. We exist in an evolving world. If hate is a learned behavior, then it is up to us to change the lessons we are teaching new generations.

It's time for new traditions, new outlooks and new perceptions.

If your words are thoughts that can enact change that is brought about from your actions, would it not be worth the effort to make a world that all people, races, creeds, ethnicities, genders, and the like can thrive in?

We are the problem, people.

Thank God we are also the solution.

What we allow to recycle will grow new disregard for moral decency. Before you teach your eggs the traditions of old, reflect and remember to add a large dose of who you are, why you are and how you became who you are in with the lesson, so they, too, can learn to walk the path your steps built.

It's now your legacy that requires your outlook, perception and determination to leave this place better than when you found it.

Before you beg and pray as you watch the news unfold the world we are existing in, dont just sit and holler, "Fix it, Jesus."

Take accountability and remember, friend:

Change begins with you.

Chapter Two:

To The Pair that finally grew in & the famous last words.

Shoop in a kiss in the Land of Peas.

The blood sport of cockfighting is real. Two roosters bred for aggression and bad things, encouraged to fight to the death is the truest explanation of how life was with the hens in our lives. It wasn't always chaotic at first.

It also wasn't always about who had the prettiest feathers.

Definitely not about who's coop was better than the roost.

From what I could surmise in hindsight, it was more about foolish pride than any egg laying in those days.

One hen in particular prided herself on being the best hen clucking, despite the awful truth everyone secretly knew. She was beautiful in the classic sense.

A girly girl of a supreme pecking order.

She was outgoing and an extreme life of the party. Truth be told, she matched her chosen rooster to perfection. They complimented each other. The typical 80's representation of a couple.

An updated version of a younger Ozzy and Harriet with feathered hair and hopeful ambitions.

It was easy to mistake them for true lovers found within one another.

To understand her movements, you must first understand his.

He was a thick rooster to say the least. He worked endlessly on himself as his ego was always at the forefront of every decision he's ever made in life. He had to be the best. The virgo within him wouldn't allow him to settle for almost greatness.

He had ambition driving him to be the best version of himself back then.

The rooster who identified with good time Charlie

wrapped up in Southern realizations.

It was all very drawn out and dramatic.

From what I understand now, he had to have her. She had another, but that didn't matter.

As Eggy has always told me, "the way you get them is also the way you lose your rooster, so be mindful of how you acquire your gent."

Shoop in a kiss.

That's allegedly where it is.

She was a sought-after hen with many options when it came to suitors.

Popular is what the old hens would say.

I later found out popular meant favored in a loose connotation.

Gotta love how the older crowd raise a vibe while turning a phrase.

I had never truly paid much attention to them until the day there was a huge commotion at Eggy's house, where these two were nesting. They had moved into a room in the back of the house that was actually the den of the house at one time.

Those two took it over, added a door and presto!

Instant master bedroom.

I couldn't have been more than 12-years-old when this whole thing was unraveling. Laying on the bed in the room I often shared with Eggy, I was watching TV when I heard the screaming disturbance. My ears perked up immediately when I heard the beautiful hen's accusatory tone.

"I didn't mean to hit him with the truck, but he had what was coming to him," she cried, allowing her whimpers to escalate.

"What!?" I whispered, placing my hand over my mouth.

Scandal on a Saturday.

I sat up on the bed, turning my head to glance at my reflection as I listened closer.

"I know good and doggone well she didn't say . . ." I whispered, getting off the bed.

Poking my head outside of my door, I closed my eyes as I tried to will myself to have superhuman hearing abilities. This whole thing was scandalous as Eggy didn't normally have such an event penciled into her quiet evenings.

Her rooster was usually drunk, laid out across the bed with the Spanish channels on blast. Eggy was usually either doing the dishes or some chore she had to have done right then. I never asked her why she did things. She had this whole system of how life worked in her home.

The woman never sat still for more than a few moments.

When I couldn't hear close enough, I tip toed down the hall toward the kitchen. Quickly poking my head out and back into the shadows, I observed the distraught hen sitting at the rectangular kitchen table being consoled by Eggy.

"Did you kill him?" Eggy breathed, moving the hen's hair out of her face.

Shaking her head no, she wiped her eyes as a cascade of tears continued to stream.

"No death. This is a good thing," I thought to myself, crossing my arms as I leaned against the hidden corner I stalked from.

"What even happened?" Eggy inquired, taking a

seat in the chair stationed across from the hen.

"Well, we were drinking," she breathed, shrugging her shoulders as her head fell.

"Obviously. You two are full of good decisions. Then what?" Eggy fumed, rolling her eyes, scoffing.

"Honestly, I don't even remember. It happened so quick," she managed, standing up quickly as her rooster walked in.

"She hit me with my own truck, ma," her rooster exclaimed, stomping back toward their room from the backyard.

"Well . . . what did you do to get hit?" Eggy countered, rolling her neck toward him.

I let out a small laugh as her expression made me bowl over. Leave it to Eggy to ask the important questions in these parts.

She didn't ask if he was okay.

Didn't quiz him to find out what he was even doing outside of the vehicle to begin with, let alone be stationed in front of his truck with this deranged hen of his choosing behind the wheel. She didn't even give him the once over as she would regularly, which meant Eggy was pissed beyond words.

It wasn't a response that was expected, but it was one that was present and accounted for.

"I didn't do-" he started.

"At least I took you to the emergency room. I could have backed up and hit you again," the hen squawked, interjecting before he could finish his lie.

At that point, that's what he was good for.

Lies.

He could charm the scales off a snake with one

flash of a smile. Eggy must've known what she had. All hens know what kind of eggs they lay.

That much I am sure of.

"Save it. What did y'all tell the police?" Eggy pushed, standing up from her chair as she yelled after him.

"She told them that my hat flew off my head and that she didn't see me because it was dark and I ducked," his voice explained.

I stood there confused in the shadows as I tried to piece together what was really going on. My young mind wasn't equipped to understand the throws of passionate blows or why someone would hit someone else with a car on purpose.

I never did get the full story on that instance, but that was the first true time I saw both of these people as they truly were. To me, they were my idea of perfection, where the guy falls in love with the girl of his dreams, marries her, works hard for her and they lived happily ever after.

If they couldn't make it work, who could?

She hit him square in his tail with a Ford Ranger.

If that isn't toxic love…

It wasn't until the next interlude that I realized the rollercoaster of relationships starts slow but escalates quickly when you have two passionate beings fighting for each other, with each other in order to keep up appearances.

They both hailed from the land of the Goonies.

They would never say die.

Not if it meant that their chosen crowd would find out that their toxic kingdom was completely fabricated, finessed, and filled with poisonous secrets. Fault has a serious truth streak that goes unclaimed in the land of these two. Neither one wants to take accountability for where they broke each other. The damage these two inflicted on one another was definitely a defining moment in my life as my young eyes witnessed what love should never become.

I realize this now.

Not understanding the real state of their relationship, I idolized them at a young age, wanting the same adoring relationship for myself one day. I thought that is what love looked like. At such a young age, I only had a few examples of what love should look like. Cheating was a whole vibe with the chickens in our family. Dramatic chaos and turbulent waters in a sea of lies often streamed high within the relationships that peppered our family. Things would happen.

Hits would land. Cheating would be realized. Affairs would be revealed and yet, they stayed together, claiming to work out their issues for the greater good of their family.

If they ever left, it wasn't for long.

One way or another, these toxic roosters would find a way to surface back into the welcoming poisonous feathers of the hens they mistreat with disrespect.

Now that I am older, I realize what love should never be.

It wouldn't be long after they married that the hen was caught cheating at an actual hotel room. I am not sure who cheated first. The way these two peas in a pod worked, it was always one trying to out do the other. If he cheated first, she would show him how she would cheat better.

Childish antics.

The lot of them.

The one thing these adults never realized is that children, though they are expected to be seen and not heard in our family, have ears and a long memory just like elephants.

We may not speak on the happenings we witness for fear we'd get the stuffing knocked out of us, but rest assured, the truth always surfaces.

Be careful of how you treat those young ears listening.

The hen ended up getting fired from her job as it was allegedly her boss that she was with. Thinking of it now, I don't know what the guy looked like. I'd like to think he may have been a good-looking stranger who knew how to wear a nice pair of Wranglers, but at this point, he could have looked like George Costanza.

I don't think it was about the person at that point.

For all we know, dude could've been a warm body used like a Nerf dart to the Velcro heart of the unhappily married.

It wasn't long after that instance that the rooster got his turn in the follow spot, publicly on full display for everyone to see. He had no more reasons to hide as it would seem.

He was gonna show every crevasse of his tail on prime billing.

Our city had this big festival that everyone in the city would attend. It featured food and wine of the world, bands, beer, and good times as the locals had a sit and visit in a night on the town.

I am not sure why these two would go out without one another in the first place. You get married to never be alone again. A single becomes a pairing. You're supposed to give up single pastimes. You give up the "me" to become a "we".

Otherwise, what is the purpose of being married?

These two geniuses.

Either the drugs were damaging his forethought abilities, or the beer soiled his cognitive reasoning, but this rooster decided to get gussied up in his Garth Brooks inspired attire to have a night for the history books.

I like to think that he thought he was that slick not to be caught. Knowing how he thinks now, I surmise that he told himself there were so many people at this fest, there's no way she'd find him out.

I have never understood why men cheat.

Does it make them feel inferior and awesome to maintain the guilt that goes along with the secreted dirt?

Why not just leave if you are unhappy?

Selfish.

God doesn't like ugly.

Everything that is done in the dark will always find it's way to the light and when it does, you better hope you have on clean panties and your hair combed as you will be forced to take accountability for your actions.

As it turns out, the hen happened to be entering the festival as her rooster was leaving the festival out of the same entrance with his new chick tucked in the nook of his wing.

It was a scandal, honey.

Eggy later told me that the hen was so pissed, she tore the Garth Brooks shirt clean off his torso in the confrontation of the century. I would have given half my ovaries to have been present and accounted for at this reckoning, but I'd have to settle for the second-hand toxic city chisme with the rest of the peanut gallery.

It was never revealed what happened to the chick. Last I had heard about it was that she had a French poodle hairstyle, gawdy earrings and a big butt with a tiny waist. Her complexion was dark, acne ridden, not pretty in the face, which was surprising as the hen he was hitched to was beautiful with a fair, pristine complexion.

None of the happening between the toxic twosome made sense.

They had their ups and downs, but none of them would register with me as life changing until a few years later when I was present for the fireworks.

It is often said that we are given lessons to learn until we receive the message within the lessons that are taught. If you don't get the lesson, you repeat the cycle until you do.

I think that's what's happening with these two. A repetition of cycles unlearned spanning over a lifetime.

It was clear these two never listened to Eggy and it showed.

She may not have had it all figured out being in her own personal hurricane, but the woman did have her insightful moments.

Around this time, I started staying at the hen's house to baby sit the one child they had at the time. The hen wasn't always kind to me. She was often rude, cold, and very stern. Mean just to be mean at certain times as if it wasn't okay for her to remain kind in her spirit. She was proud and conceit filled as she always made sure that everyone knew she thought she was better than they were by actions.

Shoop in a kiss in the Land of Peas.

The neon blinking memo that she missed was that she wasn't better than anyone at all. Not even a smidge with the state her every day life was in.

If she believed it was so, she was delusional.

She always made it a point to keep up appearances of a happy wife who had the extreme love of her husband. Truth be told, she never really had his love.

He settled for her and she knows it. That has to be hard.

He was destined to have a life that would be touched by fame had he went forward with his promising singing career. Instead, he stayed home to get married, even after he allegedly tried to pull out of the wedding two weeks before the actual ceremony.

From what we were later told was that he was forced to marry her by an overbearing busybody who didn't know her place, guilt tripping him into the marriage because of the money that was put into the wedding.

Everyone has choices to make.

He made the choice to settle and cheat.

The day I saw the true version of the rooster was one I will never forget. It scarred me for life as it made me realize that anyone can be pushed to the limit of their sanity and unless they make the active choice to change and break the cycle that he learned from his own egg donors', then his own son would also learn the toxic streams of unacceptable behavior and what love should never be.

There weren't always bad times between them. They had some times of happiness, appreciation and acceptance. Not all days were bad or indifferent, but this day.

This was the day that sealed the truth of their

relationship in my mind going forward. As a teenager, I was supposed to be obsessed and boy crazy. I should've only been concerned with how to do my hair and whatever else was happening in my chaotic existence.

Marriage counselor was not in my job description.

It still isn't, even when the hen continues to place me there.

I was laying in the back room in the dark, listening to the radio as I hummed along with the current Tevin Campbell song of the week. Laying on my back with my legs pressed against the wall, I sang along to the song until I heard a loud sounding crash followed by a huge thump.

The baby was yelling excitedly along with his father, the rooster, as he threw his hands up in the air. Running to see what was taking place, I picked the baby up and took him to his crib in the other room.

The hen and her rooster continued to quarrel with him shoving her against the wall forcefully. He had had enough of the spite she was throwing at him that day. I can't recall what the argument was over but knowing her, it was probably something to do with her nagging him about things he may have forgotten to do.

She was huge on the nagging.

Remember- no one is as perfect as she- *in her mind.*

She was ironing his clothes as they got into a shouting match for whatever reason. By the time I ran back into the room with my heart racing, the rooster was screaming two inches away from the beautiful crying face of the hen, threatening to burn her with a hot iron.

Typical hot-blooded Latina, the hen snarled as she growled back, daring him to burn her face.

"I swear I will burn every inch of your face. Then

no one would ever look at you again," he growled, holding up the hot iron to her face.

She refused to give in an inch.

"Please! Don't!" I screamed, crying as I tried to remove the iron from his hand. "You need to stop! You are hurting her."

The struggle continued as she continued to fight back as her anger took over. The panic within my young soul quaked as I tried to find anything that would snap him back into the now from the dark places his mind was swimming in.

"You're gonna end up just like your sperm donor. Eggy's future. That's what she has if you continue on. Is that what you want? You're beating her just like he beat Eggy all those years. Don't you see that!?" I screamed, fuming as tears streamed down my face. "That is what you are showing your own kid. You think he wants to see his mama all beat up like you saw Eggy?"

That did it.

I saved her beauty that day.

It was a messed-up situation to say the least.

That was them.

It was how they allowed their relationship to evolve.

I decided right then and there as my own evil egg donor came to pick me up from their house that I never wanted to have a man who would raise his hand or a hot iron to my face that way.

I was afraid to leave her there with him.

Not because he would've done something further to her, but more so because her mouth had a sharp way of writing hot checks her tail would never be able to cash. As messed up as it sounds, his behavior that night was not his true character. She had a way of bringing it out of him, just as many of us have a way to bring out the worst in some people.

Their idea of love stemmed from years of subconscious programming of abusive tendencies. Sad but true.

He never did hit her again.

That never stopped her.

I would return to their home within a few weeks once their issues had cooled. When I did return, she confided in me about the stash she was building.

"I caught him," she mentioned, opening her filing cabinet.

"Caught him doing what?" I countered, opening a window.

Pulling out the long file, the hen placed the file on the bed, opening it as she pressed her lips into a hard line. It was a file filled with all sorts of items.

Worn lipstick.

One plastic gawdy looking earring.

Receipts.

Items that were pushed down in between the seats of his truck, placed for his wife to find.

A line was drawn in the blood-stained sand between blood and water.

She should have never put me in the middle of that.

"What are you going to do with it?" I asked, searching through the items.

My mind convalesced on what sort of woman wore plastic, cheap earrings to flex to begin with. Her chosen color of dusty rose pink was way too dark of a lipstick for her to be wearing, if it was the same woman from the festival.

It was a tacky color for her.

Deep down, I like to think she knew that.

"When it is time, I will use this in our divorce. I'll get everything," she breathed, closing her file quickly to return it to its categorized hidden location as we heard the front door close.

She was better than me.

If I knew he was cheating, I probably would have poisoned his food until he shat all over every item he owned.

Over the years, the couple continued to keep up appearances, dancing like destined partners at friends' weddings as if all were well in the land of the toxic peas. Their toxicity continued to thicken as they involved themselves in the messy lives of their beloved friends, judging them as if they are above it all.

What's done in the dark . . .

We knew what to expect of these two peas. Eggy had gotten to the point to where she couldn't stand the hen any longer as her snarky, overbearing toxicity began to pour into every ounce of Eggy's home.

Allegedly, the house the hen and the rooster had was lost because the hen didn't have the rent money and didn't tell the rooster until it was too late. They lost the house over a very fixable situation, so they returned to Eggy's home temporarily.

A temporary situation that has turned into years of never leaving permanence.

Eggy has been reduced to her tiny master bedroom as the spite filled, bitter hen has taken over Eggy's home. I didn't realize things were as bad as they were until I returned home to Eggy's while I was visiting from out of state. The room I had once had in her home had been given to an ungrateful, spiteful teenager who doesn't have the manners I was raised with.

As my luck would have it, I got to sleep on an air mattress in the cold kitchen like the queen I am. Be jealous, world.

Eggy's house was old school.

The kitchen is outfitted in this orange Spanish tile that has been the same since the cooling of the Earth's surface. It has no central A/C or heat. If you want a breeze up in that house, you either sacrifice a donkey to the Gods for a stiff wind to greet you or you buy a fan that someone will steal from you after you fall asleep on any given night.

You'll start the night out sweating out the good food you ate at dinner only to freeze half to death at 3 a.m. It is the perfect balance of Hell.

There is no in between.

The night was cool, and I was deem in a glorious snoring rem cycle when I heard her whisper.

"Muneca."

Opening my eyes alarmed, I released a concerned look in her direction. She was hovering over me like she was observing my burial plot.

"What!?" I managed, scared half to death.

"She called," the hen reveals, shaking his phone as it continued to buzz.

The hen nodded her head toward the front sitting room, answering the buzzing phone.

Exhaling sharply, I wiped my eyes wondering if this was the price I'd have to pay to stay in Eggy's house for the duration of my visit. While I was always down for the scandalous messy chisme when I was broken, I didn't exactly know if I wanted to uncork this particular cheating monkey from his bottle.

He seemed super comfy in there and I was exhausted.

It always happens when you are clocking the best zzz your life has to offer.

Poking my head into their bedroom, I saw the rooster snoring a deep roar in the center of their bed. It seemed like he was so comfortably sound asleep that he didn't realize his phone was missing.

Rookie mistake #135, 867 in his life.

She's always known every single thing he's done.
Every sidestep.
She knew adulterous thought.

At this point, it was like the rooster had a definite disregard for his hen's intelligence. This was no stupid chicken he chose. She was thee sly hen of the roost with a few moves of her own. She knew exactly what his number was and is not afraid to dial that number.

Hot iron in face be damned.

The next day when the hen stepped out to the grocery store, I seized the opportunity to explain the situation to Eggy. She in turn gave me every inch of the toxic 411 involving their ever-evolving telenovela.

"He doesn't even hide it anymore. He thinks she has no idea. Mr. Slick. I won't have her getting my house in their divorce," Eggy fumed, pointing at me with a sharp kitchen knife as she peeled potatoes. "Does my life mean nothing to them? Did I not suffer enough?"

"I don't know, Eggy. Maybe he's not thinking about all that," I say, shrugging. "She can't have your house. It's your house."

"I won't be alive forever. He's going to get my

house," says Eggy.

"Fair enough." I add, turning my gaze down to the floor.

It seemed like she didn't understand that we weren't automatically privy to all ten seasons of her travesty. People learn by example. If you never speak of your trauma, it stays alive within you, festering as it continues to feed on your sense of self.

It's those examples that enforce whether or not they replicate the exact toxic energy that has been infused into their own spirit for years. Most use the experiences to shape their outlook as to what they never want in their own relationships going forward.

Others use this learned behavior as a springboard of permissions to maintain and do the same. Where they end up on the side of the fate coin resides in their chosen actions.

The hen could have let that sleeping dog drown, waking him up to quarrel ending 25 years of marriage as he is caught dirty dog red-handed. It would have been the finest comeuppance of a wake-up call that would have ever been dealt in their existence. He would have been a stuttering mess of a cheating scoundrel, especially with the girl he left to meet on the sly calling his personal line.

She should have left that crowing rooster to be drawn, measured and quartered.

Part of me pictures what that might have looked like.

He's never been a brave soul to face getting Kentucky fried head on.

While I don't feel sorry for her any longer as she chooses to repeat her toxic cycles, I want her to win for the sake of being a strong woman. Just once I'd like her to do something about the man who is ruining life as she knows it.

Life hands you these nuggets of glory that set the scales of righteous balance even. It's up to you in the end if you take the opportunity to set someone straight.

I see her waking him up with a generous slap on his tough, leathery skin. He sits up, choking on the air he was in the middle of breathing in. His eyes wild with terror as he glances around the room, trying to figure out what is happening and where he is. Glancing down, he clutches his chest as he tries to gather himself as she starts in on him immediately.

Her hands tremble, shaking as she throws his phone at him as it rings again. His jaw drops, slightly askew as his eyes narrow as he identifies the blinking number on his phone.

Clearing his throat, he stands up.

Turning to face her, he questions why she had his phone to begin with. His anger builds, wrenching out of the darkest crevices of his dirt filled soul. He pushes further, interjecting as she begins to explain that he was dead asleep, and it woke her. He inquires why she answered his phone in favor of letting it go to voicemail. Pulling on his pants, he turns to release a disgusted glare of unrealized disappointment as she continues to yell and scream about the woman she's already talked to.

Her accusatory tone giving every inch of her life into every ounce of truth that escapes her broken heart. She explains how her love for him has changed her, darkening the sweetest parts of her where love is struggling to exist within her. She breathes murmurings of "why can't you's" in between the sorrow-filled whimpers she releases.

Her soul is broken. He's broken her and betrayed her for the last time.
The hen pulls out her prepared bag from underneath her side of their marital bed. She's given up trying to turn herself inside out for him. She's held her weight to his ideals of wife perfection. She's given him beautiful eggs and what she considered a decent life. Kept his secrets when his truth should have been revealed in order to set them both free.
The hen is ruined beyond devastation and he knows it. The rooster is too busy perching on his pride to see the result of his broken actions.
He is a master of deceptive behavior. He's learned how to ace the lazy Susan wheel of accountability. It's no longer about what he's doing, done or why someone who is not his chosen wife is calling his phone. It doesn't matter what he's been out there doing in these streets.
He's not accountable. She answered his phone.

HIS phone.

The audacity.

The sheer nerve.

Life is over for her. He now has the upper hand. It's his turn to lay the guilt on thick like mayo. It's a done deal. He will feast on the toxic energy that now correlates between them.
Anything to take the steam off him and place the hot iron onto her.

She'd start crying, breaking down as she apologizes, claiming that she thought it was important because the person kept calling. She just didn't want him to miss an opportunity.
That's all.

Shoop in a kiss in the Land of Peas.

Her foot slowly pushes her bag back under the bed, allowing it to simmer like an eager hot rock for the next time he would break her into shards of glass once more. She'd give in like a sinking middle cake, crumbling with every second as the heated intention wins.

New defeat, old cycle repetition.

Chapter 3

Bullet Dodged.

The Unfit Master of The Universe

They say divine timing plays a part in every aspect of our lives in order to keep us aligned with our destiny. At this particular point in time, I can't help but wonder if the time keeping Angel who keeps watch over my particular clock drinks.

When I left home for the service, I didn't know many things that young ladies of my age should know. My egg donor was so tightly wound yet closed off to the ways of the world. In hindsight it is clear that I was one unprepared egg.

This is one of those instances in life where you just wish you could control, alt, delete that joint. Even as I write it out, I can't help but laugh and cringe as I release highly pitched… "really? Really, though? Truly?"

I mean, I can't even… but, here we are. Unstuck and reflective in all our former Toxic City glory.

In order to understand the journey, sometimes you have to reflect back at the right turns we've taken that lead us to east Jesus nowhere. It's often fun there. They have hole-in-the-wall type of fabulous eatery establishments, complete with indigestion and bad decisions that were super fun to do, if not once or twice, but several times over.

It's the best worst decision season of your life.

You cringe, wither just a little, and laugh at the same time.

The shit is hilariously painful.

Why is it that there is never a quiet moment in your evolution that your higher self can slap the sense God gave you back into you right before you commit self-sabotageable level murder?

UH.

God bless me.

Nonetheless… like a scabby band-aid, boo.

Here we go.

That most unfortunate day. There I was… a young fledgling walking into reception to begin that new, exciting endeavor I signed my life away for. Shameless admission: I had a huge thing for that one actor in Sandlot.

Don't come for me. You loved him, too.
Benny the Jet.
I heard he was changing and saving lives as a firefighter on the other side of the world.
Sadly, our union has yet to be glorified.
Moving on.
So here comes rooster 1.5.
Rooster 1.5 had light hazel eyes, brunette hair, and if I am being 100, he was like a micro mini version of my teenage crush. The Cuban version. To this day, I am still not all the way sure with what happened that day.
I remember meeting that rascal.
It was like one day he just showed up and attached to me with his mismatched yoke self.
This rooster was a conundrum. He was Cuban, yet he spoke with this backwoods country twang from a state I cannot reveal as it will identify him immediately.
He wasn't what I expected.
There were no aspects about this rooster that spoke to my inner hen. Not one character trait that was it for me.

This was purely vanity driven. I admit my brokenness was emerging from the depths that day. There were other options available to me. I see that now, but at the time, my eyes must've been hellbent on finding all the wrong solutions to the road love stood at the end of.

Needless to say, I now understand what Bugs Bunny meant by taking that left at Albuquerque.

Some folks just have to try all the wrong turns before the right one can be revealed.

Mountains, not valleys.

With the loveliness that was my dysfunctional kaleidoscope understanding of what love truly was, I can say today, I know what love is certainly not.

This was not love. Not in any aspect of this relationship.

At least, not for me.

For me, it was like I kinda…*sorta*… in some way cared about him. Not for him as a person, but I cared about him as a human being. I didn't want anything bad to happen

This was purely vanity driven. I admit my brokenness was emerging from the depths that day. There were other options available to me. I see that now, but at the time, my eyes must've been hellbent on finding all the wrong solutions to the road love stood at the end of.

Needless to say, I now understand what Bugs Bunny meant by taking that left at Albuquerque.

Some folks just have to try all the wrong turns before the right one can be revealed.

Mountains, not valleys.

With the loveliness that was my dysfunctional kaleidoscope understanding of what love truly was, I can say today, I know what love is certainly not.

This was not love. Not in any aspect of this relationship.

At least, not for me.

For me, it was like I kinda…*sorta*… in some way cared about him. Not for him as a person, but I cared about him as a human being. I didn't want anything bad to happen

Don't come for me. You loved him, too.
Benny the Jet.
I heard he was changing and saving lives as a firefighter on the other side of the world.
Sadly, our union has yet to be glorified.
Moving on.
So here comes rooster 1.5.
Rooster 1.5 had light hazel eyes, brunette hair, and if I am being 100, he was like a micro mini version of my teenage crush. The Cuban version. To this day, I am still not all the way sure with what happened that day.
I remember meeting that rascal.
It was like one day he just showed up and attached to me with his mismatched yoke self.
This rooster was a conundrum. He was Cuban, yet he spoke with this backwoods country twang from a state I cannot reveal as it will identify him immediately.
He wasn't what I expected.
There were no aspects about this rooster that spoke to my inner hen. Not one character trait that was it for me.

to him. I didn't want to break his heart, just
as I didn't want him to break mine.
Just in case said rooster reads this, it wasn't
all you on your own. I take accountability for
my side of things. That's what this whole
thing is for. Your toxic eggs might be a little
too scrambled.
This is one way for me to give you closure.
I need for you to know that.
This one just was what it was. While it may
have been majestically magical for you, for
me it remains only a small moment in time
for two lost, broken souls.
The only difference was I didn't know my
windchimes were broken at the time.
If his heart were able to decipher the music
that played, he would've known it would
have never worked.
This rooster was an enigma. He was forced
artsy in a way. For a girl of 18, he seemed
like a great deal. If only I knew then…
He came sniffin' around the reception hall I
happened to be in when our paths crossed.
Kindness often disguises itself in the darkest

places. Nearly 21 years later, my memory blacks out when I try to remember exact details about the first encounter.
I believe he crowed hello, and I said hey.
Stupendous.
A lot less glitter in the coconut than I remember, but all stars shimmer right.
I'm not necessarily proud about this first "adult" relationship, but it's like watching a movie in reverse as you question motives on key actions as the music box ballerina twirls.
Adult. Grown. Seasoned.
I think tf not.
I was out the house. Sure.
Successfully survived boot camp, hazing, and life up to that point. Absolutely. If I am being honest, it's like I was just checking things off of a shallow list filled with empty bucket list rejected experiences.
What I have come to realize now outweighs any of the things I knew then.
Just to set the record straight, I had never thought about doing it like the pigeons.
Never had an inkling to allow anyone close

enough as it was drilled in my head that I was "dirty" since age 6 by my egg donor. Told y'all she was a winner.
The only time anything remotely close had happened in said sector was a high school boyfriend snuck into my room when he was thrown out of his house. I hid him in my room. The raving mad hen flipped tf out when the neighborhood drunk called to let her know he saw him sneaking into my room.
Why he was staring at my room to begin with- that's entirely another issue, but the snitch got his eventually, so I have been told.
Nothing happened other than a few smooches.
The hen got super pissed, yelled, and screamed as she violated my privacy and even finger swiped a la Memoirs of a Geisha style to prove to her ridiculous self that I was still a virgin.
When she saw I was, she punched me with a closed fist in the face, a common occurrence in my house hold.

The Unfit Master of The Universe

I don't care how many times she apologizes.
Don't care how many amends she tries to
explain her side of what she believes is truth.
That was just one instance of many
numbered wrongs she has committed.
This egg donor should have never been
allowed to have children. Not in this life or
any other going forward. I've forgiven her,
but I will never forget what she's done, how
she's acted, and the words she has sewn into
my spirit. She knows what she has done.
For the entirety of my immortal existence I
will still proclaim the same sentiment about
her:
She is the worst human being on the face of
this earth.
That night, I was told a plethora of things
including the Hispanic fan favorite, "you're a
Roman Catholic".
As if that even matters.
That's another book.
Back to the toxic mantra at hand.
Checking off my little list, I wasn't
concerned about doing something that was

considered a sin by someone else's understanding of God. I wasn't plagued by the same mentality. Somewhere in my mind, I was curious at best, but not really intrigued with things.

This rooster, on the other hand, had other ideas.

I've seen plenty of movies in which the first time was equal parts wonderful, disastrous, exciting, nerve-driven, and horrible. It wasn't horrible in the same way you are thinking.

"Oh, the first time is always the worst. It gets better. Keep doing it."

Um. Hard pass, Pedro.

This experience was horrible because it has forever ruined Heman for me. The powers of Grayskull will never be the same.

This rooster should be plucked, tarred, and feathered backwards for ruining Masters of the Universe for me.

The jerk.

10 minutes, grunting, and Heman.

The Lord was clearly testing me.

Thinking back on it, I was numb, bored, and

unmoved in my spirit. The world didn't move. Louis Armstrong was not singing. There was zero Whitney Houston Dance with Some-damn-body vibes.

There was no magic.

Nothing except Heman lifting his damn sword in victory.

If anything, I was more confused than ever. This rooster was off flittering his wings in lovely pastures, and I was going through the motions, unsure about life in general.

A few weeks went by with the rooster fairly quickly. He had a plan. His leg quarters were primed for pegging me in a trapped cage. His egg laying days were ticking, so he wanted a hen that was going to give him what he wanted.

Security.

Longevity.

Possibly a padded cell.

The more I got to know this rooster, the more I realized that he was more unscrambled than I originally thought. What he was convinced was loved turned to one-sided obsession.

Before long, I couldn't breathe.
It got to the point where I would borrow his car just to go home so that he couldn't follow me from the base to my family home 250 miles away.
There were noticeable differences in his character that told me I was not in the company of a gentleman caller. We weren't together very long before I noticed he wasn't raised right.
The toxicity became his blood type as his love language became silence.
Watching a movie, I had the sheer nerve to fall asleep. The audacity of me to be chasing adequate rest. The betrayal of my conscious to be well-rested.
When I woke up, the rooster sat his tail down next to me, perched as he shoved hamburgers in his face. He brought nothing for me.
This small, assholey action spoke volumes that countered his silent love language. That was the turning point for me.
Like all Texan women, if you actively choose not to feed me-

The Unfit Master of The Universe

To eat without me…
To eat in front of me without offering me a bite…
I could give a damn if I was sleep.
This small-minded act told me this rooster was on borrowed time in my life. His actions to feed himself and not the woman he supposedly loved to the point of obsession showed me he was unworthy of my attention, my worship, and my love.
If it was only once, then I would accept it as poor home training and manners.
This happened over and over again.
Selfish.
I was told by a card reader the egg donor frequented as I was waiting for her that I needed to beware of a man with green eyes. Not believing her, I shook my head and said "okay", thinking it was this rooster who was a full cob short of a full harvest. He had hazelish/green eyes.
The crazy seemed to fit.
Over the next few weeks, I began playing hide the clock. A pregnancy scare put things

in perspective exceedingly clear for me. At the March Madness event his unit was having, I was talking on the phone as one of his unit mates came over to talk to me asking what I was doing dating someone like him. I find myself asking myself that same sentiment even as I write this thing out. He was blessed to have someone like me. Deep down, I think he knows that which is why he could have been acting out further.
I broke up with this rooster over 15 times. Toxicity, party of two.

If you ever want to know how to break up with an obsessed lover, let me know. I've done them all. None of them got through to this chicken. He kept coming back. The only difference being that he was acting as the scorned obsessed girlfriend in a groovy barracks drama that won no acclaimed applause.

It was giving very much lifetime Candice Cameron/obsessed love vibes and I was so not here for it.

The big fireworks that lit up the sky

came the day the egg donor had gallbladder surgery. I had a blissful moment in the sun over the lapse of three weeks. That earned silence was pure bliss.

Those weeks gave me the freedom I needed to breathe and just be young to experience.

Imagine the shock and surprise I was met with when I walked into the recovery room to find the egg donor on the phone with a whaling rooster who was begging her to order me to go back to him.

Again.

Selfish.

A few weeks after that incident, his chain of command called me in to discuss why I wouldn't date him. When I explained, they shook their head agreeing and let me go on about my business.

Sometime later, I was told he was ordered by his commander to stay away from me.

This particular rooster ended up dating, then marrying a bigger lady, who was mean to him. Don't feel too bad for this chicken.

He forced her to perm her hair to match mine, and also (allegedly) forced her to get lip injections to make her lips shaped like mine. When I say this dude has serious obsession issues, I mean he needs professional help, a team of behavioral therapists, and a boat load of Jesus to get him together.

I have never been so happy to walk away from this form of toxic love, but at the same time, I wouldn't have known better at that time if somebody would've given me a clear, precise map to victory drawn in crayon.

I had heard from this roosters a few years back. He was working for Sprint and let me know immediately that he was happily married. The woman was still perming her hair to match mine, and when I said that I was happy for him, this rooster had the nerve to berate me over his children. Both of his children were special needs. According to this rooster, he was still exceedingly angry with me because he deeply felt that his children wouldn't have been "special" if they were from me.

Furious, I gave him a right piece of my mind as I reminded him that it is a blessing to have these babies regardless of the circumstances. I reminded him that he should be grateful for having any kids at all with the way he is. The conversation ended shortly after that as he began hollering and I had too much to live for than to sit and listen to a hollering rooster with no head.

Last I knew of this poisoned fowl, he was on Tinder, but seemed to have better luck as he was looking for a second shot a la' Tila Tequila.

Toxic bullet dodged.

Chapter 4

Um...No.

The Fallen King with Bells On.

Every King has his day with the sword. It's not necessarily how they fall that makes the measure of the crown that rests on his head. Many times it is their road to ruin that determines the measure of the man for years to come.

I should have known the first time I saw him that he was going to be absolutely not worth his weight in the amount of salt he tried to spread across my path.

For the record, I wasn't old enough in the mind to be dealing with this type of guy. Hell, even at 40, I am still not ready for his load of tactical bullshit. At 19, it wasn't like I had a whole bunch of boyfriends to begin with.

My egg donor wasn't exactly graceful enough to allow her eggs to have a sort of a normal life. We will put a serving fork in her rotisserie destined self later.

I could pinpoint my doom down to the hours I paced back and forth in the parking lot during a March madness event on post. At the time, I was dating unfit rooster number 1.5.

I call him that because I am convinced he was two chromosomes away from a full egg. One evening with this rooster and you, too, will see that they weren't one of the eggs that got the full hour under the incubating heating lamp.

This was that sort of egg.

Rooster 1.5's disclosure in chapter III. We won't relive that madness here. This is about a new chapter that truly should have never been written in my book of woe.

Beware of the man with the green eyes.

If only I would have listened then.

This red rooster wasn't worth the trouble he dealt me, just as he wasn't worth the love I invested in him. He was, is, and will always be toxic. He doesn't know how else to be. His family never taught him what unconditional love is, was, or could be.

A little background to give you insight to a smidge of his toxicity.

He's one of two. The story I was told was that he was a twin. His egg donor put some black magic on her rooster and the pinch backfired, making her lose one of the twins. The little chick that remained was spoiled and celebrated beyond belief, simply because he was the only twin left.

As he grew up, he was forced to be an adult to make decisions and care for his two other siblings while the egg donor went out, drank, and gave in to her demonic vices. She carries a black magic "pouch" to make people bend to her will (allegedly), which matches her appearance. This woman is taller than a normal woman would be and dark in complexion with black hair. Her body is shaped like a square box that has been beaten in delivery, which speaks loudly of her extracurricular activities.

The lipstick she chooses to wear doesn't compliment her skin tone as it is a shade she should never consider in her wheelhouse. The lavender pink hues do nothing for her appearance. When I met her, she had acrylic nails on her toe nails in a French.

She is completely insane, evil, wicked, and vile all in one sitting. The demons that remain attached to her are numerous and because of her actions, cannot be removed by anyone in life.

There is a reason she will never know true happiness or peace.

She has earned every ounce of the trouble that will

rise up in the road to meet her. She has earned it for more than the next ten lifetimes to say the least.

This particular hen did not realize that when she does certain things, those things come back to her generations times ten, beginning with the one she loves the most, her rooster, then each of her chickens. She did all of this to her own blood. That's not even the saddest thing.

Pure dumpster fire trash from the inside out.

You will see why.

Back to that glorious day March Madness wreaked havoc in my existence. I was talking on my Nokia standard blue phone, bored out of my mind when the red rooster approached. His face beamed with a mischievous smirk at the ready as he approached and began talking to me. The sun was shining so bright that I didn't see his emerald green eyes immediately as his eyes were squinting.

We conversed briefly as he inquired about why I was dating rooster 1.5. I laughed, shaking my head as I reiterated that my little rooster wasn't as bad as he thought.

A silver blue '65 mustang caught my eye as I turned my attention toward it. It had a pearl white interior with white wall tires.

She was clean, shining, and apparently the key to my heart.

Later that evening, my roommate and I were having a hurricane party as a tropical storm cut through the city. The downpour was generous and a prime setting for the ill-fated love that would destroy my existence.

Refilling my cup with Malibu and pineapple juice, I was kicking back talking to soldiers who were coming in and out of our room as we blasted music. Lost in conversation, I was laughing as a male soldier was telling me the story about his latest conquest, a norm among the group we were in. He held my attention with his tale of dating woes gone wrong as my roommate began screaming for me to come to the door.

As I popped my head out to see what she was yelling about, she nudged her jutting chin in the air as she pointed downstairs. Walking out onto the stairway, I moved to get a better view.

We stood staring down toward the ground floor as this red rooster paced back and forth, glancing up toward our balcony every so often to see if we'd notice him.

"Look at this tap dancer," my roommate whispered, gesturing toward him.

"It's pouring out. What the hell is he doing?" I replied, taking a sip of my drink.

My roommate shrugged, scratching her leg as she continued to bob her head from side to side along with the music that was thumping. We watched him for a full five minutes as he continued his pacing. We had never seen someone legit draw a line in the sand in an effort to be noticed with such tenacity before.

As my roommate and I exchanged knowing looks, I began laughing as we both screamed, "shotgun". Victorious, I smirked as I did a small celebratory dance.

Growling as she gritted her teeth, my roommate stomped off back into our room.

"I'm getting wasted tonight. Bring on the tequila," she proclaimed with her voice wavering.

Shaking my head, I turned my attention back to the pacing

red rooster.
"Hey," I yelled out.
My roommate poked her head out of our door to watch the interlude.
"Hi," he smiled, grinning up to me as he released a three fingered wave.
He began talking as he placed his right hand on the nape of his neck as he dropped his head.
That should have been the sign that I was way in over my head with this one.
"Wanna come up?" I yelled down, pointing to my room.
With a nod of his head, he rushed up the stairs to greet me.
"Hi," he whispered into my ear.
His voice was like the passion you think resides within the darkest brand of whiskey. Warming, burning with feverish intention as it claims your soul in one swallow.
Every part of me wanted to be wanted by this guy. He had this way about him, secreted within the smallest drop of arrogance that remained his addicting allure.
"Hey. Welcome. So... what are you doing tap dancing in front of my home?" I asked, taking a sip of my drink. "Do you want a beer?"
"Sure," he nodded. "I...um. I was hoping you'd see me."
The boldness in this rooster.
My soul saw him before I walked out of my room.
That much I remember.
"How can anyone miss someone pacing back and forth in front of their balcony?" I laughed, shaking my head at him.
I stared at him for what seemed like decades as I noticed his eyes were emerald green.

"Well, I wasn't just going to barge in without an invite," he added, taking the beer from my hand.
"It's a hurricane party. That's what one does," I exhaled, glancing over to my roommate who was lost in conversation with a guy she considered repulsive. "Are your eyes green?"
"Yeah," he confirmed.
That should have been the moment I bolted, but my heart said otherwise. Stupid heart. Pump the blood.
Over the next few days, we were inseparable.
I found myself excited to get off work, knowing that I'd see him. The one problem I encountered with him was that he was in the same unit as rooster 1.5. The little scorned two piece short of a biscuit was hellbent on making existence hard.
The red rooster was so different. He was confident to the point of a comfortable conceit that seemed to dangle over his exterior. I had never dated anyone like him before. This particular rooster was so invested in his appearance, how he smelled, how he spoke, and how he carried himself. He was charming and very gentlemanly. If you consider someone who is dressed like a GQ model come to life right in front of you, you, too, would question your decisions in life.
We had met on a Sunday, but by that Friday, the teasing nature of him seemed to peek out from beneath the surface.
I liked the idea of him. He seemed to fit all the small vain boxes I had mentally collected for rainy days when one considers who they want to be attached at the hip with. If I only knew then...

That Friday night came quicker than expected. We got off work and planned to get together to go into the city to a club I had frequented as a teenager. The way this rooster was acting seemed off. He was a little pissy, giving attitude filled clap backs to every single thing I would say. My eyes connected with my roommate in knowing glances as we both considered what was taking place.
Honestly, I was furious inside. I didn't know who this dude thought he was acting out of pocket all boastful like he was. He seemed exceedingly arrogant as he continued to dish out commentary filled with painted scenarios about how he was going to go get "all the eligible swans" this particular club had to offer.

"Go ahead. No one is stopping you," I snapped, rolling my eyes.

"I will. Don't you worry," he scoffed, checking his reflection in the mirror as we pulled into the parking garage.

As he parked, I whispered back and forth with my roommate as we tried to figure out what his damn problem was. We weren't sure why he would act as he was. It's like his confidence was on shaky ground within the 2-hour car ride into the city.

I knew I looked epic. I dressed effectively for the evening as I wore a small black skirt, a spaghetti strapped black top with beaded designs peppering the shirt, paired with black stilettos. My curly hair was pinned to perfection in an updo. I wore dangling earrings that elevated my ensemble. It was a whole high dollar Barbie look.

The rooster wore a white guya vera type of shirt with black slacks and dress shoes. He looked great.

The Fallen King with Bells On.

If only his mouth could stay shut and stop ruining the vision for me.

When we got off of the car, I reserved my tempted anger for another moment as I interlocked arms with my roommate in an effort to ignore the boastful rooster. We snickered amongst ourselves as we planned how many guys we were gonna dance with.

Less than a block away, I gasped in horror as I realized that I forgot my ID in the car.

"Y'all go ahead. I'll be right back," I revealed, getting the keys from my roommate.

"You're not going anywhere," the rooster commands, following me.

"Yes, I am," I reply, rolling my eyes at him as I turned to begin walking away from him. "Go get your girls. Wouldn't want them to be neglected."

I picked up the pace as I marched up the block.

The rooster rushed, picking up the pace as we got closer to the car.

"Would you stop!?" he screamed, grabbing my hand.

We stopped right next to a building that had reflective blackened glass.

Positioning himself behind me, the rooster placed his hands on my hips as I crossed my arms.

"Look at you," he began.

Rolling my eyes, I scoffed. I was in no mood for his clever musings or narcissistic views of his world. If he wanted to run off and remain Captain save-a-hoe, I was certainly not going to stop him.

"Why would I go after anyone else, when I have you?" he continued, kissing my right cheek.

I'd like to say that my 19-year-old self didn't fall for his lines. I'd love to say that I told this wonder muffin exactly what he could do with his choice words, because I wasn't in the market for a chump dressed in shiny tin foil.

I'd like to say all that jazz.

Unfortunately, his brand of bull worked on my "19-year-old-never-had-a-true-fully-functioning-sauve-boyfriend" self.

That was all it took.

Lord, if I could just go back to that moment and double kick myself in the chin and tell that version of me to "run like hell in the other direction."

If only.

After that night, we were a thing.

Four months after dating, he asked me to marry him in a round about way. It was like a conversation and then an understanding. It wasn't magical. It wasn't what it should have been at all.

Things were going swimmingly until they weren't.

It didn't take long for my Prince to turn back into a frog. Before long, I started to see little things, changes that trickled in along the way.

Now that I know what I know now, this jerk was down his own false champion narc program with no return in sight.

We were fine some days and horrible together others. He became flawed right before my eyes. It began not to matter what the main issue in our day was. He was determined to place me right under his thumb.

On one of our shopping trips, we passed by a well-known jewelry store. Browsing, I came across a tear-drop sapphire that was just meant to be mine. The thing about this particular ring was that it was something I wanted to do for myself. It wasn't about the purchase of the ring, but more about the meaning.

I saw this ring as a gift of self-love to myself. A gift from me to me. It had zero to do with this guy. After the life I had already lived up to this point, I wanted to buy the ring for myself as a first big purchase.

This infuriated my frog.

I didn't share why I wanted the ring. Didn't give a whole elaborate thought process to include him in my madness. It was my business.

Naturally, we got into a huge argument about the ring.

If I were gonna give him more credit than what is due, I'd rationally say that he probably wanted to purchase the ring for me.

In hindsight, that's how this jerk works.

The essence of a guy that was so addicting in the beginning of this love adventure became the ruins of my capital. Gone was the addiction to everything he was in my life. The GQ model was no more. His façade melted away, leaving behind the naked, unpolished version of who he was pretending to be. What was left of him was no match for the memory he remained. The man he turned out to truly be has zero originality, limited imagination, and if the truth is willing, he's the sort that takes credit for other people's achievements while expecting to be praised like he's some prized pig that won the fixed fair.

Hottest toxic mess. Party of 1.

During the argument, he screamed that it's not that

he wanted to buy the ring. It was more than he said, "no" and in doing so, he didn't want me to have the ring.

For a Texas woman, that is a no-go. If you were to tell me "no", especially at that age, I will do it out of spite. I wasn't and still will not let any man rule over me. The only one designated for that primed position is God.

We argued and fussed at each other until it was time to go to dinner with my roommate and her new boyfriend, which turned out to be a friend of my boyfriend. I sat through the rooster flirting with every waitress that came to our table during dinner with my new ring on my finger at a popular restaurant.

Livid, I couldn't believe how he was acting.

The sheer audacity.

After I confronted him about how he was acting, the rooster stood up and decided to walk out on me at dinner. Following him, I cried, trying to figure out what was wrong with him. Grabbing his arm, he forcefully pulled away from me. I fell backward, slipping on the loose gravel as I was wearing heels.

He laughed and reached down to help me up.

That should have been another sparkling, shimmering flag of no, but I was too blind to see the holes in our relationship.

No man should ever laugh when the woman he allegedly loves has tears streaming down her face, let alone falls backward, hurting herself due to him pulling away.

Even as I write this, I am hurting for the girl I was then. I'm not even close to the pain this jerk unleashed in my life and already I am beside myself with empathy for the things I could not see.

The Fallen King with Bells On.

I should have let his ass storm off like the toddler he still remains to be. In that moment, I should have ran in the other direction.

Should've, could've, would've.

The things revealed to the unseen.

There are highs and lows in every relationship. I wondered if the state of my relationship was my payback for rooster 1.5. In trying to make amends by being friendly, I reached out to rooster 1.5 to no avail. He was just as delusional as I remembered, if not worse. All the interaction did was show me that the right choice was made to walk away.

Sometimes there are moments when the right thing to do is nothing.

A few days later, we were hanging out as red rooster was tuning up his car when I made the mistake of joking with him.

"What if I was pregnant? What would you do?" I asked, releasing a side glance at him.

I wasn't pregnant. At least, not at that moment. He did not like that question at all. It wasn't like there was something I was hinting at or even a moment of wishful thinking. It literally was just a moment of I wonder what he'd do.

Back then, I always wanted to know things about him. I wondered what he thought or why he did certain things the way he did. It was my way of getting to know him. The way his face shined when he explained his life through memories was addicting, even the memories that hurt him the most.

His favorite uncle came to visit, which he prepared

me for. He was so worried about me getting to know his uncle and as we went out to dinner, his uncle seemed so kind. I found out later that this was an intel mission, and the uncle was definitely not kind, nor should he ever be trusted. He went back and reported his findings to the evilest person alive next to my own egg donor...

His egg donor.

As our luck would have it, his unit got tasked to go fight the fires in Oregon, when the fires tore through the state. My rooster was terrified that he would not return to me, so I took off my Jesus coin necklace that was blessed by the Pope. It was the one possession that meant the most to me as it was a gift from Eggy.

"It will protect you, just as it has protected me. You can bring it back when you come back into my arms," I smiled, placing it around his neck.

I kissed my frog as tears streamed down my face and just like that, he was deployed.

During this time, I threw myself into the gym. I tried not to think of him for fear that it would somehow overshadow his protection and good luck, so the gym was the one way I knew how to take out my frustration. When I wasn't in the gym, I was working or hanging out with my friends from back home or even my roommate.

I had zero time left for any funny business.

Two weeks into his deployment, I received letters and phone calls from my rooster when time permitted. He sent photos of him in his cute firefighting uniform. He looked like a mixture of tired but courageous and brave.

In that moment, I felt blessed and happy to have someone who cared for me the way he claimed he did. I thought that the rough patches we were going through were normal, character building experiences that we would get through. Somehow I knew that if we could get through this together, we could get through anything.

One morning after PT, I began to feel a bit strange. I wasn't sure what the issue was. Nausea that seemed to be related to a drinking situation, yet I had not drank any alcoholic beverages.

When I wasn't at the gym, I was working. When I wasn't working, I was at home talking to my rooster. There was no outside interference. There was no extracurricular activities or visitors of any kind.

I was lovesick over my rooster.

So I thought.

As I woke the next morning, I ran to the bathroom, heaving over the love I considered my everything.

With two blue lines, I confirmed my rooster's alleged fear.

I was pregnant.

Staring at my roommate, who was furious, I silently freaked inside.

My roommate was upset because she wanted babies, but for some reason, any time she got to the third month, her body would let go of the baby. Terribly sad for her, naturally.

Hindsight- how dare this Trollope. Taking my moment to be upset because of her situation. If the envious stiletto fits...

Not knowing what to do, I waited until I talked to my rooster before telling anyone else. That night when he called, he sounded so loving and excited to speak to me.

"I've got... I'm pregnant," I blurted out.

I was told he almost passed out, but when I finally got something out of him, he seemed excited and happy about the baby. He was due home in a few days, and I was excited to see him after a few months of separation.

When he returned, everything seemed like it was a romance written in the stars. We were happy in our bubble until I had to tell my egg donor what was happening. As we were getting married, I didn't see it as a bad thing.

I saw it as a blessing, being that we would be building our family- a little in reverse. It wasn't a moment of, "oh, my God. We are Catholic and sinners." It was a blessing to me.

I thought of a little piece of eternity made of me and him that would be part of our legacy. Our little family.

As we were cleaning up his room, my rooster caught me off guard and said that we needed to move off post in our own apartment now that we were going to be starting our family.

What he didn't get, just as I am certain he still doesn't get to this day was that we had already started our family. He and I. Him and me. We were the start of our family. At least, that's how it should've been.

We moved into our new place and to be honest, he was 25 and I was 19. Baby leading baby, really. We were both learning as we go.

Life was moving fast.o

We used to go out to the club and hang out with his friends, but when you are newly pregnant, that is not something you want to do. Your body is busy building eternity a home. The last thing you want to do is go clubbing.

This rooster.

There are many things I've had to forgive him for over the span of 21 years. Many, of which, I also had to forgive myself for in the road to healing. This life is supposed to be the most epic of learning experiences designed to shape us into who we are supposed to be, just as it is meant to make us grow.

As my baby was growing inside, the rooster would be furious that I was gaining weight. When I asked for chicken nuggets, a fight would ensue and often end with, "you're getting fat".

"I'm pregnant… remember?" I'd retort, feeling more and more alone with each passing second.

Deep down, I hated that I constantly had to make that declaration like I was constantly having to renew my line drawn in controversial quick sand.

"You never want to do anything. Let's go hang out," he'd growl, furious with my need to rest.

"You go. Go have fun with your friends. I need to rest. The baby is taking a lot out of me," I'd sleepily reply.

That was my first mistake. You'll see why soon.

Over the next couple of days, we were hanging up laundry when he said, "I want to be a bachelor forever."

I remember turning around to look at him and wonder what the hell he was actually thinking.

"Except that you're not a bachelor and we are getting married and have a baby on the way, and…" I reasoned, shaking my head in disbelief.

This fucking guy.

Like I said, the red flags aren't red with this red

rooster. They are sparkling in red glitter, just begging to be read at a high volume.

As if that wasn't bad enough at where we are in this tale of woe, I feel the need to explain how this rooster carried himself. The rooster I knew carried himself as if he was the rule of the roost. He spoke exceedingly smart and eloquent with insightful musings at times.

There was never a moment that he didn't look impeccable. He wore Aqua Di Gio, a heavenly scent that had to have been created for him. The top notes in that potion just did his whole existence a conjured blessing.

He was confident in every aspect of his life. His walk revealed that to anyone who saw him coming.

Imagine what a shock that was to find out it was all an act.

For the first few months of my pregnancy, we had decided to keep things hushed from friends and family until after we were married. I wasn't sure why he was so adamant about that at the time, although I know better now.

He tried to explain his mother to me, failing to reveal the idealized nature of who she truly was. We were driving around, I can't remember what for, and he blurts out, "do you know what Santeria is?"

Releasing a confused look at him, raising a brow towards him.

"Do you mean like the Sublime song?" I quipped, making him laugh.

"Yes," he smirked.

"Why?" I countered.

The whole conversation was strange. We were

closer than ever, about to bring our little person into the world, yet having a conversation about this magic nonsense.

The tangled webs we weave.

"I've seen some things. Things that can't really be explained, and I am trying to figure out a way to ..." he started, searching for the words to reveal hidden truths.

"Explain?" I added, watching his every movement closely.

"Exactly," he exhaled, gripping the wheel as he pulled into a gas station.

"Just tell me. I am listening," I confirmed, smoothing out the hem of my dress.

"Okay, babe. Be right back. Want anything?" he smirked, turning off his car.

"Gummy bears," I smiled.

"You got it," he breathed, exiting the car.

I sat in deep contemplation as I tried to piece together what he was about to reveal. I've never been someone who was ever involved with anything dark. The most I've experienced with the things people considered dark arts at that point was the tarot reader my mom frequented, the same woman who tried to warn me to stay far away from the man who I was now attached at the hip with.

As a devout Roman Catholic at the time, I wasn't familiar with any of the things he would come to speak on. I wasn't lying when I asked naively about the Sublime song reference. I was so brand new then.

Then. Not now.

Later that day, the man who had my heart

explained to me that his egg donor was into what he considered "dark shit". He spoke of an instance where his uncle went missing and the family was in total disarray, so his egg donor and her egg donor threw "something" at a mirror and the mirror went black. He claimed that within minutes, an image showed his uncle was tied and blindfolded to a post in the middle of a field and that they were able to find him. As if that wasn't a cause for caution, he then told me how he was actually one of an original two, but his brother died because his mother did "something" against his father and that was the outcome.

The rooster enlightened me about a lot that day, and he wasn't holding back when he explained in detail the true character of his egg donor. He revealed how obsessive his mother was over him and even stated that if we visited during Christmas, I as his wife, would probably have to either stay on the couch alone or possibly at a hotel while he would be at home with his mama.

Yes, I said what he said.

Oedipus complex in reverse de la chingada.

My rooster was terrified to tell her about our baby, just as he was afraid to tell her that we were getting married. I didn't understand his fear. I probably should of.

My egg donor was a prime obsessive, helicopter asshole, too.

The kindness within me didn't think he was selling me the name brand products. I somehow convinced myself that he just didn't see what I saw. I didn't see this situation as a fail from the jump before the first foot on our path had been planted.

I saw this as a growth opportunity. I didn't want

his egg donor to think she was losing him. I wanted her to be grateful she was gaining family. Her son's family.

The southern traditionalized toxicity that had been programmed within me said that if this man loved and respected his mama, then he was sure to respect, love, and honor his chosen wife.

I couldn't have been more wrong.

First, before we get into the juice, this guy has no idea what love. Just as I had no idea what love is, should be, or what love should feel like. The toxic traits that exist in his family were threaded deep within him, which he had very plainly revealed to me, so I can't fault him for me not picking up on it then. If I am being bold with dashes of honesty, I think he still clings to the same traits in his current crumbling marriage, which further tells me, he still has no idea what love is, and he has learned no lessons in this existence. That truly is sad for him.

His track record tells the world exactly who remains at fault, but this is about our story, not about his row of broken hearts, 4 wives, and 9 children with different women. Routine of toxic behavior is proof in the proverbial pudding. He reaps what he sows in the world. God is making sure of that.

This is about our journey together and the failure of love that mixed with the success of toxicity claims.

When he finally did tell his mama, it didn't go down like it should. She flipped and had a full-scale meltdown. She allegedly had to be taken to the hospital to get Ativan to chill her ass out because she literally could not handle her son getting married.

She later spoke those exact words to me when I

finally talked to her.

My rooster gave her my work phone number for her to contact me.

Worst mistake of his existence to that point.

As I was pregnant, I was removed from road work as a working Military Police officer and placed as a secretary of our PMO SMG. He was so kind. As I am not naming names in this retelling of my woes, I am sure he knows who he is, even if he doesn't realize what he did for me in this time.

This official person became my voice of reason when the world was not so kind to me. He was lenient and exceedingly kind. As I was supposed to be overseeing his office, I was not supposed to be getting any personal calls in. The one exception was only family emergencies.

Imagine my surprise when I answered the phone to find the rooster's egg donor on the other end.

She quicky identified herself and explained that she asked for my number so that we could get to know each other now that I was going to be in the family. She spoke exceedingly quick, burning through a lot of topics as I agreed, trying to get her off the secure line.

Without missing a beat, another hen, his aunt, the woman who was married to his favorite uncle, took a moment to ask if I was even strong enough to be in their family because, "the women in their family had to be strong enough to pull themselves up by their boot straps."

I sat staring at my reflection in the framed Army poster that hung on the wall across from my desk as I held the receiver to my ear.

I couldn't believe what I was hearing. This trollop actually wanted for me to feel sorry for his egg donor and how she was not handling life well. Like this was somehow my issue to deal with because "I was the cause".

The fucking toxic filled audacity and nerve.

The hen went on to explain that his egg donor does things when she is not in her right mind, which further told me she was someone not to be trusted.

Again... HUGE sparkling flag.

This hen began calling every 5 to 10 minutes on the encrypted line, which was supposed to remain open to receive calls from the office. Non-stop calls about complete and utter nonsensical bullshit.

That's what she was calling for.

My first impression of her was that she wasn't my type of people. She was pushy, mean, and cold. She had no respect for herself or others and clearly had zero respect for her son, his future wife, or our union.

When I got home that night, I asked why the heck he gave his egg donor my work number. He claimed she wouldn't stop until he did right then, so he gave it to her.

Again- this is the type of man who does things and expects everyone else to clean up his messes.

Does it truly surprise you that he went against what I told him in the first place?

Over the next week, his egg donor continued to call and harass me to suit her needs while I was at work. I started to converse briefly with her to answer whatever she wanted wedding wise. She continued to ask me questions as if she was actively trying to get to know me and in return, she'd tell me things she wanted for her son and how he was used to doing certain things.

I'd yes her to death to get her off that encrypted line.

Even after I complained to my rooster, and he constantly told her that I can't have calls at work, she held true to her "do what I want" attitude.

After she stressed me out to an inch within my sanity, I talked to my rooster at length, reiterating the need for us to keep our baby a secret until after we were married. If his egg donor was having this sort of reaction to our marriage, it was clear she was in the midst of having a "hand that rocks the cradle" issue.

He agreed and we both did what we could to deal with the brewing storm that was his mama.

Four days before our wedding, we went to get the marriage license and hand in our paperwork. The rooster took it upon himself to enroll me in his unit as his wife and get the process started for the family care packet process. We would be getting paid for being each other's spouse, so we figured every little bit helps. Excited about everything we did, he even changed our outgoing message on our voicemail to greet the world with:

"You've reached Mr. and Mrs. Rooster. Please leave your name, number, and purpose and we will get back to you shortly."

Generic but concise and to the point.

We didn't have much in our apartment at the time.

A couch, a table, a bed, and the TV he had in his room. We were just starting out. Like many new couples who just jump not things, we didn't have an outpouring of riches.

This apparently struck a nerve with the rooster.

The Fallen King with Bells On.

Somehow in the darkness of his mind he seemed to think that he is entitled to things he has never had to work hard to earn and thinks that he should be given things. Toxic traditions are hard to break.

That much I am aware of.

Things continued to get more and more stressful. He'd get angry over the smallest details and even berate me as I sat on my knees scrubbing our floors to get the scuffs from our polished boots out. The true mess of who he truly was began to surface the closer and closer we got to the wedding.

There were so many sparkling flags, I should have been smart enough to notice instead of enjoying the damn light show.

The rooster was adamant that he had to go with me to pick out my dress. Even when I protested that it was bad luck to see me in my dress before my wedding, he boasted, "we are already married. How can that be bad luck?"

When I found the dress I wanted and the attendant placed the veil on my head, he became enraged and kept on nagging me to go eat because he was famished. Throwing him a bag of chips, I purchased my dress upset with him because he took that moment from me.

The closer we got to the date, the more unhinged he became.

I began to have second thoughts and second guesses at answers I should have remained strong on. Taking the rooster home to meet my father's family proved the turning point for me. My jitters had my feet iced cold and damn near falling off, but still I pushed forward.

He continued to press me about my weight, giving

me the "good girl" dog pats when I did my leg lifts because "he could not have a fat wife".

Fat. *Not pregnant.*

I was a size 10 at this time. If you threw corn in my direction, it would fall without touching me. Waist was snatched even at 3 months pregnant, yet all the rooster saw was that I was fat and should be ridiculed and disowned because HIS baby craved Dominoes pepperoni deep dish pizzas, meatball subs with extra pickles and chicken nuggets on command.

He continued to comment how obsessed he was with Gwen Stefani, a blonde waif singer with no curves, who was popular at the time. God bless her.

I was Hispanic, brunette hair with curves for days featuring an athletic figure, boobs, and a snatched waist.

Cue the sparkling flag.

Pregnant but not showing, I continued to keep my little secret hidden as I walked hand in hand with my rooster as we walked up to my father's grave site.

"This is the man I'm going to marry, pop. I love him," I whispered, closing my eyes.

I breathed deeply and for a small second, I felt like I was doing the right thing. So I thought.

As my rooster let go of my hand and walked back to the car, I bent down touching my dad's tombstone as my intuition kicked in.

Pulling my egg donor aside, I told her that I had the feeling that I shouldn't marry the rooster.

"What do you mean? I thought you were sure. We already paid the hall," she growled, grabbing my arm.

"I don't know. I was talking to dad, and something

is telling me not to do it. I think dad is telling me-" I explained, getting cut off rudely when my explanation fell short for her idealized world.

"Listen. You are just having jitters. You'll see. You'll be married, and it's all..." she equivocated, glancing back at my rooster sitting in the car.

Grabbing her arm, I shook my head as my eyes filled with tears.

"You aren't hearing me," I breathed, sucking in air. "He's mean. He tells me things about my weight. He's not loving . . . anymore."

The rooster released a concerned look toward me.

"You're just stressed. Tired," she replied, pulling away to walk towards the car.

We got back to the house in record time. Exiting the car, I ran toward the house. Hitting the bathroom, I puked my internal grief into the toilet as my egg donor fawned all over the rooster.

He watched me puke with such disdain dripping from his expression. That wasn't the face of someone who truly loved the mother of his unborn child. Even as he questioned me about why I was puking, like it was something I could control, I wondered what was becoming unwired within his mind.

It's like he was regressing into his childhood essence with each passing day. Before long, there weren't any aspects of the man I grew to love. What was left behind was not so shiny anymore. There wasn't anything I wanted from him, and it was causing me deep, traumatic anxiety as I tried to confront the truth that was bubbling beneath the hidden surface.

The question that continuously flexed in my mind was:

"Is this who I see myself spending eternity with?"

I couldn't answer that one question, and that is what was plaguing me the most.

"Do you really love him or do you just like the idea of him?"

I do know the answer to that question now. At the time, I didn't. There were so many issues that were tied into the two pinnacles we stood on. I lied to myself more in that era of my life than ever.

I told myself that I could love us enough for the both of us. That was one mistake upon many. As far as what I knew about love from the toxic examples that I had seen growing up told me that this is what love was. My understanding and my intuition were in war with each other.

My heart kept telling my rational mind that I was doing the right thing. We just had to get through this bump. A huge bump that was standing in the road painted in neon right as we were beginning a failed union that was already in progress.

It was a disaster pie.

Either way you sliced it, I would be the one getting hurt.

That much I knew.

My roommate at the time began pulling away further and further because the jealousy and envy was too much for her to bear. She forced her then boyfriend into marriage. I later heard that she only did that to prove she could do something I couldn't at that stage in my life. The joke was on her, and she had disaster pie all over her dress as her marriage didn't last... so I was told.

The fire you kindle for your enemies, right?

The day finally arrived when his family and I would finally interface. It was the day before our church wedding. The rooster prepped me over and over with what to say and what not to say around his family. He explained how I'd love his father because he looked just like him and they were alike in many ways. He attested that his sisters might be a little standoffish but once they got to know me, they'd love me too.

One looked exactly like him. It was creepy.

He claimed that she had this thing about her face and how her skin was so important to her. She would damn near kill anyone who even made a move towards the pillow she slept on, so he prided himself in stealing it from her when she was around.

The other sister was the kinder of the two. He laid out her whole life for me and detailed her shy personality to being the harder to warm up to.

"She's just... different, yet the same," he breathed, glancing around the airport.

"Whatever that even means," I shrugged, smoothing out my dress.

At this time, my small pregnant belly appeared to be the same sort of tummy one could have after a generous meal on a skinny woman, but more noticeable and apparent depending on what I wore.

For this first impression/meet the in-laws extravaganza, I wore a dress that had brown scales of checkers with sensible loafers that I was in love with. I had styled my hair down, curly with generous product. Honey, a stiff wind didn't stand a chance with that hair. I added a pink hued lip gloss and that was me.

I was exceedingly normal. No flair or overdoing anything.

After we waited for two hours, my rooster became increasingly more nervous with every passing second. He kept reiterating every rule he put in place as if he was the one double checking the luggage that kept what was left of his mind.

"And... don't breathe a word about the baby. I am not playing. I want to do it a certain way," he advised.

"Message received. I won't say a word," I smiled, knocking him a kiss.

When another hour passed, I suggested that we split up to look for his family as the airport was huge and people often get lost. Knowing what the looked like, I was sure I would notice them in the crowd. As I searched, I practiced in my mind how I would greet them and tried to decide if I should hug them or not.

I was so nervous but excited and a bit concerned to find out what state his egg donor would be in.

As I was 19, I had never been put in this position before. I didn't have in-laws. Didn't know what to do with them. Did I feed them or ...?

The jury is still out on that issue.

Luck would be slapping me in the face sooner than expected. I spotted my rooster's family and walked behind them as I tried to catch up. I was in listening distance when I heard the mad hen say, "I don't care if he loves her. She is not marrying my son. I won't have it. I'm here to bring him home. He belongs with me."

I was shook, stunned, and all the things.

My soul jumped out of my body and asked, "did this bitch really just...?"

"Yes. Yes she did," I thought to myself as if I were answering the poisonous thoughts of my soul.

She really did.

His father, ever the supportive rooster, cowered to her by answering a simple, "yes, dear."

I cleared my throat and said, "excuse me."

They all turned around, stunned by my appearance. Extending out my hand to shake her talon, I found the small amount of courage I maintained for such a moment, smiled kindly and opened with, "hello, it's nice to meet you. Now I can put a face to the woman behind all the phone calls."

Her alarmed eyes looked me up and down before cutting her wild blackened eyes back to her husband with a knowing look.

She smirked and nodded her head as my rooster came running to hug her. Instantly, her disposition changed. One could cut the tension with a sharpened razor. It didn't take a sooth seer to see what was happening was going to be no good for our future. His sisters looked so scared.

As the rooster made his way around, greeting his family, I made my way over to his uncle. His uncle's reaction told me what I needed to know. He acted like he never met me before, refusing to shake my hand, or a hug or give me the time of day.

His clock was broken the day he went back with bad

intentions.

My rooster was overjoyed, showing me the homemade strawberry cake his egg donor made for him for his "bachelor cake". It was a shitty looking cake with a childhood picture on it. I didn't say a word about it as I figured it had something to do with a sentimental thing made by his mama. If it made him happy, I wasn't going to get in the way of that.

The rooster began singing and dancing with his mama, looking over at me as he said, "that they were going to tear up the dance floor like no one has ever seen."

I sat back and observed my rooster as his demeanor slowly began to change into a low life, sort of cholo, Chicano stereotype. His speech changed and his posture became different. Gone was good posture and the pride he carried himself with. It was shocking to see.

Who was this person?

One thing was for certain, two things were for sure, I had no idea who I was marrying or what I was getting myself and my child into.

The person I knew to be a certain way melted away the second he got around his family. This high class, educated, well-spoken man I had dated and created a child with was just the illusion conjured up by a low-class Chicano falsehood of a thug wannabe.

Mr. "West side is the best side" was so not it for me.

To make matters worse, his father was continuing to release calming statements to his mother as if he were taming the best within her 6' foot behemoth self. It was utter insanity. She knew nothing about me and now that I think about it, the joke was on him as well. He knew nothing about my background either.

Excited by the arrival of his family, it took exactly two minutes for the rooster to go back and break his own rules.

"She's pregnant!" he said excitedly, smiling like the cat that ate the canary.

That did it.

"She's what?" his egg donor screamed.

His sister began crying, shaking her head. She was no fool. She knew what was coming.

"It's okay. We found out after I asked her to marry me. We are starting our family right away is all. It's okay," he explained, touching my stomach.

His egg donor shaked her head in disbelief. His father looked mortified as he spoke to my egg donor apologizing for his wife. It seems that is something he was used to doing, which is an incredibly sad existence to live.

He definitely deserves a medal or a cuddle or extreme therapy.

That's for sure.

"No. This is not happening," she growled, squaring her shoulders toward me.

"But I love her," the rooster whimpered.

I stood back watching my rooster argue with his mother as he looked like he was shrinking. The more he shrunk, the higher her voice got as she was screaming at the top of her lungs in the airport. When I saw he couldn't take anymore, I grabbed his hand.

"We love each other," I said, stepping in front of my rooster.

This woman could give a shit. Love didn't live within

her. It never has. She had to trap her own rooster with Blackmagic to make him love her. He was with someone else when she did what she did.

I won't list it all here, but she knows I know what she's done. So does God, and she will reap what she has sewn into others.

"But... mom. She's pregnant with my baby," he cried. "I won't leave her. I love her."

"I don't care. Your wife is supposed to be white with blonde hair and blue eyes. She's too dark," she replied, refusing to listen.

Her son was heartbroken right in front of her by her own doing, yet she didn't care.

White with blonde hair and blue eyes.

Clearly, she was on glue. Her ass was ten shades darker than I am. I am light golden olive in skin tone. Brown eyes with a blue line that goes around my pupils. I have dimples and I've got my head on straight.

This woman is delusional. She refused to back down and even tried to shove me down an escalator.

At the end of this magical meeting, she proclaimed she disowned my rooster. She came what she came to do, as she had stated in the beginning. She broke the rooster.

As we left the airport, my rooster held my hand and we cried together as I explained that I loved him, but I wouldn't let him be disowned by her mother. I loved him enough to walk away because he loved his mama.

Mas pendeja.

I know.

Stopping at a gas station, I stood outside for a breath of fresh air as my own egg donor was furious that he chose me over his mother.

"I guess you got your fairytale," she snapped.

My own evil egg donor.

Don't fret. She gets her eggs beaten thoroughly, so I've heard.

Karma doesn't forget an address.

We went back to the hotel where my rooster cried until it was time for him to go to his "bachelor party", which was supposed to be made up of him, his uncle, his dad, and his male cousins.

As he kissed me that last time, I knew I wouldn't be seeing him again. He kissed my tummy and smiled at me. I sat up from where I was looking down and revealed the truth I knew since the day I went to my dad's final resting place.

"You won't be coming back to me. Will you?" I asked, looking down at my tummy.

Scoffing at me, he caressed my jawline with his boney index finger.

"I will be there with bells on," he replied, kissing me once more as he left for the night.

Crying, I dropped my head into my hands. I was devastated. I knew in the depths of my broken soul that he was gone for life. It was a hard realization pill to swallow.

A few hours later, I went to the rehearsal for our wedding. What was amazing to me was that all his cousins were there, but my rooster was not.

Shaking it off, I played around with childhood best friends that I had known since kinder, dancing around as his sister filmed us, which I remember thinking was odd. My friend spoke to me about making sure that this guy was always going to treat me like I deserved because I was a good person, and he wanted the best for me.

I smiled at him and returned his kind words with a huge hug. He was my best friend, who I considered like a brother. There was never any feelings of love other than a platonic friend sort of sentiment. He wasn't my type. Never stood a chance.

My friend had some sense to him. That's what made him "not my type" as I like to say.

That didn't stop his sisters from filming what they thought they saw as something else. These little bitches were dressed in black, claiming that they were attending a funeral.

They were not innocent in the least.

As the rehearsal continued, the rooster's dad pulled me aside to show me a science poster board looking project that he made up with pictures of his son. He was explaining each picture as happy moments that he cherished because he hadn't always been able to be around his son. Seeing how his wife acting, I knew why.

"His mother does things she shouldn't be doing. I want you to know that my son does things I do not approve of. He's spineless and weak against her. He is a coward, and he can't stand up for himself. Please remember these photos and see these memories. That's who he truly is. I am not proud of him," he advised, closing up the poster board as one of the cousins came out.

He hurriedly placed the project underneath the seat of the truck he was in and gave me a hug as I went back inside to rehearse.

The next morning I woke up in a panic. I paced the

length of our hotel room as I tried to make everything make sense. I kept telling my own egg donor that he was not coming, and he was going to stand me up but she just claimed it was my jitters because she was certain he loved me.

Urging me to call him to soothe my jitters, I called to find out he was leaving me. The rooster told me that he spent his bachelor party talking with his mother and he knows the baby isn't mine. He heard that I slept with rooster 1.5 and that I was untrue. Panicked, I tried to tell him that he was wrong, and I've never stepped out on him, but the damage was done. I now knew what his father was talking about.

He was right.

His son is, was, and will always be the biggest coward life has to offer.

As I went round and round with him over the phone, his mother called the church to cancel the wedding that we had set up. Confused, my priest called my egg donor as I argued with the rooster as he demanded that I give him his daughter.

"What are you even talking about? She's only 3 months in my stomach. She's mine. You can't have her," I countered, standing my ground.

"We'll see," the rooster growled, ending the call.

My priest demanded that I go in to speak with him immediately. I was already dressed in my wedding dress when the call came in. With lightening speed, I threw on a pair of blue jean shorts, a gray tee, and some converse. Speeding to the church, I tried to remain calm as I walked in to find the priest on the phone with the rooster.

"She walked out on me. She's standing me up at the alter," the rooster reiterated. "She doesn't want to marry me."

I shook my head in disbelief.

"She's pregnant from someone else. She was trying to trap me," his voice roared.

"Oh, cause he is SUCH a prize?" I scoffed, furious as I paced in the office.

His mother came to the phone to explain that her son was not at fault and that he would not be attending a shotgun wedding as her son had too much to offer.

She was right.

Her son had way too much bullshit and toxic trauma to offer anyone in this life or the next ten.

My priest. God bless him. He remains my favorite priest to this day. He argued with the rooster's mother as he pointed out that I was no coward as I was standing in his office, right in front of him and it was clear I was ready to be married.

"Well, he's not," she snickered, hanging up the phone.

The priest was so angry he slammed the receiver down, breaking the phone.

After a few seconds of silence, he hit his desk with his fist.

"That son of a bitch!" he screamed, catching all of us off guard. "I do not mean to cuss, but this situation warrants it. How is he claiming you left him at the alter when you are the one here, ready to go before God with this son of a bitch?"

I began crying as my world as I knew it came crashing down. I knew it was coming. It's like everything was happening in slow motion. Unable to deal with the moment I found myself in, I began to breathe slowly as I was escorted to the front of the church as my wedding guests filed in.

Everyone I have ever known or met up to that point in my life was in attendance. We had damn near 1,000 people there, staring back at me as I walked out to face the music alone. Turning to face the crowd, I took a deep breath and looked back at the priest who nodded at me.

"I don't know what happened. The groom has had second thoughts. I am heartfully sorry for wasting your time," I managed.

Tears streamed down my face as I was forced to present my bridal bouquet to the Virgin Mary of our church.

"I hope he gets hit by a train," I growled, throwing the bouquet down as I lost it.

I hugged my egg donor, devastated as I cried out in pain. What happened after that was a little bit of a blur. I think my soul blocked it out or something. The only thing I can recall is snapping out of the crying fit inside the crying room of my childhood church to some woman I didn't know rubbing my back telling me it would be okay.

It was horrible.

I was broken. I couldn't eat a thing. All I could do was cry. A few days went by where I was immobile. When I finally returned to my apartment, I found it picked clean.

While I was cleaning up the mess and taking responsibility, telling everyone the deal, my rooster cleaned out my apartment. He only left the bed behind with my lingerie displayed out on the surface.

When I spoke to him later, he claimed he couldn't fit the bed on the truck. That is the only reason it was left behind.

There's more to the story, like this rooster bringing a date to our divorce, his arrogant self being proved wrong as he demanded a paternity test to find out that our baby is 99.998% his, his accusations of me being a "witch", only to end up in the arms of an actual Blackmagic practicing witch who puts period blood and shit in his food—allegedly.
I'm gonna bet that has something to do with his inability to be accountable for anything in his life, his infidelity and how he might treat her, but that is another chapter for another series.

In the end, it was he who lost out. In finding myself, taking accountability and being true to myself, I learned that I did not love him. I liked the idea of him. Thanks be to God that I learned how to invest in bigger, better, more lucrative ideas.

In hindsight, I would have either outgrown him or have been forced to settle for being some unfit, unaccountable rooster's wife. Our life together would be a disaster, having to fight his mother at every turn. That's a task his current estranged wife knows very well, I think. God made me for more than that.
I would have normally never settled for second best if I knew who he truly was from the beginning.
He thinks he won, even after all these years, yet after 4 failed marriages with karmic women, the cheating, the lies, and children who might or might not be his, I would say he won the fire he kindled for me.

The Fallen King with Bells On.

I saw his picture via social media by my child, who refuses to claim him as her father. He looks like he has suffered in life. The things he and his mother have done will continue to rise up in the road to meet them as karma continues to balance the scales and all I can do is remain grateful that he was such a shitty person. I'm glad it never worked out. I'm happy he isn't my problem any longer. No one loves a toxic, unsolvable puzzle with lying attributes. He's proved that with each step of his life. I'm glad he did as he did. In the end, it saved my life.

I'd be stuck with him in a life I never deserved.

I got the best he was ever going to be while he was with me. He's proven that. He's never bettered himself or advanced past where he remains settled for bare minimum in life.

Truth be told, he was blessed to even have me in the first place.

Moral of the story: To thine own self be true.

Never, ever go against your gut. The rooster you could be crowing for may actually be a grocery store diseased pigeon dressed in prime roosting feathers.

Toxic City" Opera Omina

Vol. II

April 2022

Amaarah Gray

American Writer/Poet/Screenwriter/Producer.

Accomplished World Traveler, Speaker, Author, Veteran, 3rd Degree Blackbelt World Champion, Writer, Poet, Producer& Avid Shoe Wearer, who is a die-hard RedSox fan. In that order.

Member of the International Association of Professional Women.

Born in 1980, Amaarah launched her career as a Writer in November of 2012 with several titles under another Nom De Plume, Grayer Vaughan, exploring different avenues of storytelling. To her credit, Amaarah has penned 8 series and 25 scripts to date.

Hustle Poet Vol I will be the first book in a poetry anthology due out in 2021.

To her credit, Amaarah has penned:
The Vaughan Chronicles: Magnolia Like the Flower (2012)
The Vaughan Chronicles: Burning Blossom (2015)
The Vaughan Chronicles: Starshine (2016)
The Silent Violent Few (2014)
The Silent Violent Few: Risen (2015)
The Silent Violent Few: Noir (2016)
Chariot of Constance (2016)

The Monster Inside (2018)
The Cathedral Saga: The Receiver (2017)
The Cathedral Saga: Reign (2021)
Scissorwood Drive (Est. Release 2022)
The Jarred Heart of Amara Grace (Est. Release Late 2022)
Hustle Poet Vol. I: The Beginning will be the first book in a poetry anthology due out in 2021.
Hustle Poet: Vol II: The Continuation (March 2022)
Hustle Poet: Vol III: The Current Situation (November 2022)
Toxic City: Opera Omina Vol. I (October 2021)
Toxic City: Opera Omina Vol. II (April 2022)

Amaarah is the Creator/Producer behind:
In The Pod with Hustle Poet Podcast (2020/2021/2022)
Toxic City: Opera Omina (2021/2022)
Stories from the Pod: (2021/2022)

All podcasts are available on iHeartRadio, Spotify, Audible, Stitcher & Amazon Music.

CPSIA information can be obtained
at www.ICGtesting.com
Printed in the USA
LVRC080319111121
703047LV00004B/58